Endorsements

Charting Your Course to New Horizons is a wonderful tool developed by Colleen Sullivan to assist anyone who is interested in getting to know themselves better. Colleen's workbook provides a key to a personal journey of exploration and reflection on your life's story, past and present. It is a challenging yet empowering workbook that has the potential to change and strengthen lives for the better. For those who are feeling stuck or off-course in life, this book is a great place to begin a new journey.

—Wendy Carver, CEO
Lifeline—Harbour to Hawkesbury

This book arises from Colleen Sullivan's clinical and teaching experience in the field of applied psychology. Soundly documented and written in an engaging style, it belongs to the self-education genre of literature. It is an exceptional tool for the development of human potential. The principles used cross the boundaries of race, religion, gender, class, and culture.

—Milton Hook M.A., EdD, Sydney

Colleen Sullivan's inspirational book *Charting Your Course to New Horizons* is a lighthouse. No matter whether the ocean journey ahead is calm or rocky, a light will shine in your life.

—Margaret Wright MSc, UKCP
Accredited Psychotherapist, Supervisor, London

Colleen provides a good framework for steering candidates into making their own decisions. She knows her material well and asks the right questions. Having being an early participant in her *Charting Your Course to New Horizons*, I have no hesitation in endorsing Colleen.

—John D'Alessandri
Director/Financial Planner, Sydney

Charting Your Course to New Horizons

A Companion Guide for Group Work and
Individual Personal Development.

Explore and Discover
Your Authentic Self

Colleen Sullivan

BALBOA.PRESS
A DIVISION OF HAY HOUSE

Illustrator: Craig Ballantyne
Front Cover: Marie Theresa

Balboa Press books may be ordered through booksellers or by contacting:

Balboa Press
A Division of Hay House
1663 Liberty Drive
Bloomington, IN 47403
www.balboapress.com.au
AU TFN: 1 800 844 925 (Toll Free inside Australia)
AU Local: (02) 8310 7086 (+61 2 8310 7086 from outside Australia)

ISBN: 978-1-4525-1274-7 (sc)
ISBN: 978-1-4525-1275-4 (e)

Print information available on the last page.

Balboa Press rev. date: 11/16/2023

To
Faye and Marie Sullivan
and
Warren, Amy, and Alistair Ballantyne

Craig Ballantyne

Contents

Illustrations by Craig Ballantyne

Aurora

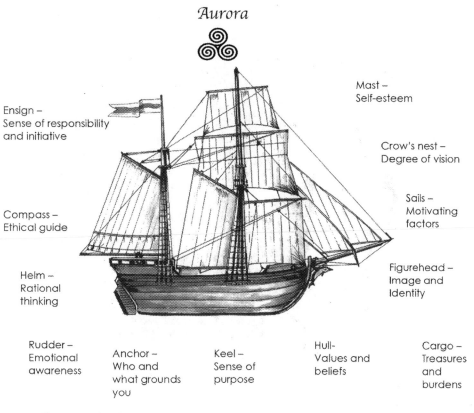

Ensign –
Sense of responsibility
and initiative

Mast –
Self-esteem

Crow's nest –
Degree of vision

Compass –
Ethical guide

Sails –
Motivating
factors

Helm –
Rational
thinking

Figurehead –
Image and
Identity

Rudder –
Emotional
awareness

Anchor –
Who and
what grounds
you

Keel –
Sense of
purpose

Hull-
Values and
beliefs

Cargo -
Treasures
and
burdens

Illustrator - Craig Ballantyne

Concepts - Colleen Sullivan

Preface

Today I had three encounters that let me know I had to write this book. They were especially profound following hot on the heels of a morning reflection. The first was an invitation by my yoga teacher, Lesley, to join a dialogue group. Her invitation was eloquently written and, in essence, expressed the idea that the time had come for those of us with different perspectives on life to share our views. She was encouraging us to create a synergy, to connect with the collective unconscious and move toward a greater love for and understanding of humanity and the world as a whole.

The second encounter was with Ginda, a very determined and dedicated artist. This was not a chance meeting but one in which it was envisaged (at least by me!) that it was I who would be giving the guidance and support. However, the situation was reversed, and it was I who was enriched, energised, and guided to take on this task. The idea had lain dormant for years, waiting to be awakened.

Then, finally, the reason for the paralysis explained in a book that Ginda gave me to read—*The Artist's Way* by Julia Cameron—made an impression. Fear! It was time to face that and simply put pen to paper and create something that I knew would not be a literary masterpiece but rather a genuine expression of a deep need to reaffirm an alternative perspective.

There is nothing new in this perspective. If you take time to listen quietly to the poets, songwriters, philosophers, and religious prophets throughout the ages, it has been said in many different languages and in many different ways for thousands of years. I am hoping to encourage you to embark on a journey of self-discovery that will raise and expand your level of consciousness through simple practical exercises. I hope that it will also enable you to pause long enough to weave some of these universally held beliefs into your own life and the lives of others.

This is not going to be a leisure cruise. If you wholeheartedly apply yourself to the process, you will be challenged in every part of your being. After many years of learning and training, I have found that it is only when we take off the gloves, roll up our sleeves, and get actively involved in questioning and experiencing life that we begin to gain greater insight and awareness—and then not always! This book is only a guide. I challenge you to reflect on what is presented and encourage you to consider what you find to be new and different. It is written with love and an attempt at humour. I hope you enjoy the journey and that it broadens your view of yourself, humanity, and the interconnections between us all.

If you would like support as you travel on your journey, please do not hesitate to contact me at info@colleensullivan.net

I wish you a bon voyage.

—Colleen

Acknowledgements

I would like to acknowledge all those who encouraged me and actively supported this project—Craig and Maureen Ballantyne, Katrina Clark, Ian Cook, Abby Dudney, Milton Hook, Janet Merton, Julian Pulvermacher, Conny Pulvermacher, Leah Sheldon, Elizabeth Starr, and Colin Welsh—for their creative and specialist input.

I would like also to thank all the participants who attended this course in its infancy and commented and contributed in their own way to make it the final product that it is.

Craig Ballantyne

CHAPTER 1
Point of Departure

Our deepest fear is not that we are inadequate. Our deepest fear is that we are powerful beyond measure. It is our light, not our darkness that most frightens us. We ask ourselves, Who am I to be brilliant, gorgeous, talented, fabulous? Actually, who are you not to be? You are a child of God. Your playing small does not serve the world. There is nothing enlightened about shrinking so that other people won't feel insecure around you. We are all meant to shine, as children do. We were born to make manifest the glory of God that is within us. It's not just in some of us; it's in everyone. And as we let our own light shine, we unconsciously give other people permission to do the same. As we're liberated from our own fear, our presence automatically liberates others.

—Marianne Williamson

Itinerary

This chapter provides an overview of where this guide and travel log is planning to take you, and how to use it.

Viewpoints

The viewpoints indicate which specific skills and abilities the guide will focus on in a particular leg of your journey. For example, in this chapter they are:
- focus of attention
- inductive and deductive reasoning
- creativity

Travel Bag

The travel bag includes a list of the resources you will require for a particular part of the journey. For this section, you will need:
- a journal
- a piece of A3 paper or cardboard
- old photographs
- magazines
- bits and pieces from around your home and garden that are meaningful to you.

Introduction

Welcome to the journey of life!

There are vast arrays of self-improvement books on the market that give guidance on how to reach your full potential. This book is different from these in that it gives you the opportunity to assess your current needs and skills and also provides you with ideas and activities to develop and practise your latent ability. This will have an impact on every dimension of your life. You will be embarking on an adventure, and hopefully you will discover and look at yourself and others in a completely new way.

This journey is intended to be full of interesting challenges, surprises, and anecdotes. You will be given the opportunity to explore (and maybe even discover) your own gifts and talents and learn how to consciously use them effectively. You will create your own paradigm or model to help you maximise your inherent abilities and to guide you in this new millennium.

You will be the captain of your own sailing craft. The model we will be using is that of building a boat and crossing tropical seas to an exotic island of your dreams, and learning to engage with other travellers and pirates you may encounter on your journey. The illustration of the craft outlines the concepts that it represents.

Travel Guide

The goal of this travel guide is to assist you, the traveller, in embarking on an adventure on which you will encounter a variety of different terrains. It is not an excursion for the faint-hearted, but it is guaranteed to enrich every element of your life. This guide is designed to help you explore your unconscious intrinsic and extrinsic motives and perspective on reality. It has been developed from life-skills training materials that I have presented over the years. It is specifically designed to challenge your mental and physical fitness and to assist you in evolving your personal sense of identity and self-esteem while fine-tuning your intuition. This is achieved by completing a number of activities and practical experiential exercises.

This travel guide has been compiled from a vast array of academic research materials and sources. Occasionally these are acknowledged within the text, but all are recorded in the bibliography.

At the end of each chapter, there is a Notes page where you can jot down any ideas, self-reminders, or thoughts that you might have.

Monitoring Your Progress

In the back of this travel guide is a list of the activities that will give you the opportunity to enhance your awareness and skills. On completion of each activity, mark and date your progress.

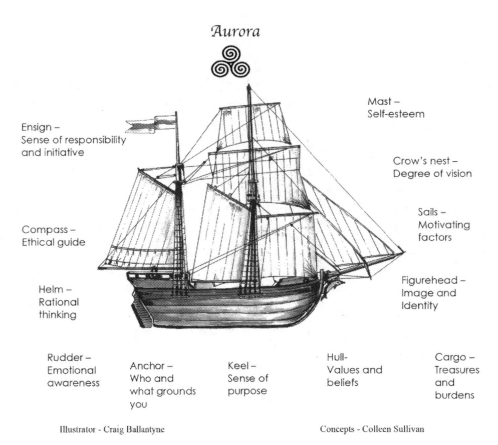

Aurora

Ensign –
Sense of responsibility
and initiative

Mast –
Self-esteem

Crow's nest –
Degree of vision

Sails –
Motivating
factors

Compass –
Ethical guide

Helm –
Rational
thinking

Figurehead –
Image and
Identity

Rudder –
Emotional
awareness

Anchor –
Who and
what grounds
you

Keel –
Sense of
purpose

Hull-
Values and
beliefs

Cargo –
Treasures
and
burdens

Illustrator - Craig Ballantyne   Concepts - Colleen Sullivan

Travel Bag

At the beginning of each chapter, under "Travel Bag," you will find a list of items (similar to a list of ingredients for making a cake) that you will need to complete the activities for that particular leg of your journey. For example, for this leg of the journey you will need a journal, a piece of A3 paper or cardboard, old photographs, magazines, and bits and pieces from around your home and garden that are meaningful to you.

Craig Ballantyne

4

If you are ready to embark on this exciting journey and apply yourself to all the activities in full, let us begin! Your adventure starts with a personal collage, creatively exploring where you are at the present moment.

ॐ *1.1 Activity: Make a Collage*

A collage is a collection of unrelated items glued to a backing in an artistic manner. Page through some of your magazines and look at the things that you collected from your home and garden that are of value to you. Either sketch them or stick them onto an A3 sheet. The collage should reflect who you are and the people, experiences, and things in your life that have brought you to where you are today. This exercise will possibly take longer than you think, so take your time and enjoy what unfolds.

Journal

The purpose of the journal is to allow you to explore freely the thoughts that continuously whirl around in your mind. You will be encouraged to write in it regularly. Your journal should be completely private. Be honest and truthful. By writing things down, you clear the way for other thoughts and ideas to crystallise; blockages are removed, allowing new ideas to come to the fore. You will be amazed by what happens when you give your thoughts the opportunity to be fully expressed and explored. Previously elusive and abstract concepts become understandable and meaningful, enabling a clearer perspective.

Date your journal. This helps you to reflect back on certain recurring thoughts and feelings and to perhaps link them to certain events. For example, my close friend Nancy found, on ruminating through her journal, that her marriage always seemed to hit a rough patch in February and June. It was an annual pattern. By musing through her daily journal over these periods, she found it always to be the same. Her schedule was wall-to-wall booked with social events. Her husband, John, was the principal of a prominent school. The busy times in the school's social calendar were February and June. She was able to understand then why, as an introvert, she felt tense and distant from her husband during these months. They were both over-committed with social events, leaving no time and no energy for their personal lives.

My friend now knows in advance that these are going to be particularly stressful times for them as a couple and, with this awareness, plans her life around them. Either she plans for her work to take her out of town at these times, or she downscales her activities during the day so that she has the energy needed to cope with the functions she has to attend in the evening. More importantly, she does not take these bumpy times in their marriage so personally. She recognises that they are simply due to outside pressures.

Craig Ballantyne

🌀 *1.2 Activity: Make Your First Journal Entry*

Make the first entry in your journal now. Write down your expectations for this course.

Viewpoints

Listed below are the viewpoints (concepts and skills) that you will visit while on your journey and a brief description of each:

- *assertiveness:* stating and insisting on your rights in a calm and controlled manner while recognising the rights and feeling of others
- *beliefs:* opinions you have accepted to be true
- *communication:* understanding the dynamics of communication within the transactional analysis communication model
- *conflict resolution:* to address, solve, and remove areas of opposition or hostility between different parties
- *creativity:* enhance the ability to be inventive and imaginative
- *decision-making:* the ability to make an insightful choice
- *deductive thinking:* analysis of the situation in fine detail. This is the ability to focus on the specific details of the situation and to record these in a rational and controlled manner. It is the ability to focus on the facts of the situation without contaminating them with emotions, values, and beliefs.
- *emotional awareness:* being conscious of your instinctive reactions and feelings

- *environmental awareness:* being conscious of the dynamics and happenings occurring around you
- *ethical guide:* your inner voice, which provides insight or wisdom to guide your decisions
- *financial management:* to maximise the use of all available opportunities without exploitation
- *focus of attention:* to focus on your life goals and the steps needed in achieving them
- *global perspective:* a worldwide perspective on life
- *goal setting:* planning and achieving personal goals
- *health:* a state of physical, mental, and social well-being
- *inductive thinking:* accurately and logically interpreting the above details in terms of accepted theoretical concepts
- *initiative:* to take responsibility for your personal situation and to act consciously and positively so as to improve it both for your benefit and those around you
- *interpersonal skills:* the ability to successfully communicate your needs and enlist the cooperation of others
- *motivation:* internal and external motivating factors
- *negotiating skills:* the ability to maximise a solution for all parties involved
- *nutrition:* healthy eating
- *rational thinking:* consciously navigating everyday situations through asking Socratic questions of why, where, what, when, which, how, whom, and what if.
- *self-esteem:* to be conscious of and embrace your own self-worth
- *sense of purpose:* the driving force—unique and different for every person—that enables and directs your efforts in a meaningful way and allows you to feel fulfilled
- *sense of self:* the degree to which you are conscious of yourself and integrate your values and beliefs in your life.
- *sensuality:* healthy physical expression
- *social awareness:* a deeper conscious understanding of other people
- *spiritual awareness:* to be aware of something greater than yourself
- *stress management:* positive coping strategies
- *time management:* maximising the use of all available opportunities without exploitation
- *values:* opinions that you have personally selected from a number of possible beliefs, have publicly declared, and have integrated into your lifestyle
- *vision:* an accurate perception of reality and the requirements of the environment

These fall into three main categories: knowledge, skills, and application leading to insights, as seen in the illustration.

Charting Your Course to New Horizons
Personal and Professional View Points

Application
Develop an Aurora model
Creative
Initiative
Sensuality

Knowledge
• Beliefs and values
• Health
• Emotional awareness
• Environmental awareness
• Motivation
• Nutrition
• Rational thinking
• Values

Skills
Assertiveness
Conflict resolution
Decision analysis
Deductive thinking
Financial management
Focus of attention
Goal setting
Inductive thinking
Interpersonal skills
Negotiating skills
Stress management

Insight
Global perspective
Sense of purpose
Sense of self
Social awareness
Spiritual awareness
Vision

1.3 Activity: Assess Your Current Skill and Awareness Levels

The purpose of this exercise is for you to create an awareness of your current position so that you can monitor and congratulate yourself on your progress as you work through the activities in the travel guide.

This is a self-evaluation. Rate yourself on a scale of 1 to 5, with 1 being the lowest and 5 the highest level of application. For example, if you don't analyse a situation and don't think of it from every perspective before making a decision, you may give yourself a rating of 2. Alternatively, if you are very careful, ask a lot of questions, and do a mountain of research prior to making a decision, you may give yourself a rating of 5. At the end of the course, you will re-evaluate yourself and determine your progress.

Viewpoint Rating:
Your Current Skill and Awareness Levels

	1	2	3	4	5
	Low				High

Assertiveness

Beliefs

Communication

Conflict resolution

Creativity

Decision-making

Deductive thinking

Emotional awareness

Environmental awareness

Ethical guide

Financial management

Focus of attention

Goal-setting

Global perspective

Health

Inductive thinking

Initiative

Interpersonal skills

Motivation

Negotiating skills

Nutrition

Rational thinking

Self-esteem

Sense of purpose

Sense of self

Sensuality

Spiritual awareness

Social awareness

Time management

Values

Vision

Developing these skills and abilities will also improve your self-discipline, persistence, and flexibility—whichever is appropriate in a given situation. Consequently, you will increase your sense of control. People who feel in control of their own destiny generally do not experience stress negatively and are healthier and more productive. They are also better able to make a decision, think logically, and accept their own conclusions. Taking control over your circumstances often simply requires a change in perception, and once this is achieved, dynamic changes in all aspects of your life will follow. Successful people go that extra mile in almost every sphere of their lives—in their interpersonal relationships, work, play, and personal development. They see life as an adventure, a challenge to be enjoyed.

All this means a lot of hard work! To embark on this journey, you are encouraged to dedicate at least thirty minutes every day to your travel guide and journal; otherwise, you won't get anywhere. It is envisaged that each leg (chapter) of the journey should take you approximately four weeks—though in truth, this is a lifelong adventure!

1.4 Activity: Consider What You Have Learned So Far

In your journal, note each of the viewpoints listed previously that you would like to develop during your journey. Consider the following:

- What specific element would you like to explore? Perhaps you could start with your thoughts and expectations for this journey.
- What insights did you gain from your collage?
- Note how you are feeling right now and about the prospect of the journey ahead of you. Are you committed and ready to walk the road and face the challenge? Or is there the temptation to shelve this book until some future date?
- Do not worry about spelling or grammar or even content. If you wish to ramble on about the routine of the day, do so.
- Acknowledge what has featured predominantly in your thoughts during that day.
- Ideally, you should write in your journal at a particular time each day—early mornings are best for some.

In the next leg of your journey, you are going to focus on who you are as a person and who you would like to be in the future. If you would like to engage in one-on-one support or join a small group with which to share your journey, contact info@colleensullivan.net.

Remember to mark off the activities you have completed at the back of the travel guide!

CHAPTER 2

Designing and Building Your Sailing Craft: Below the Water Line

Your vision will become clear only when you can look into your own heart. Who looks outside, dreams; who looks inside, awakes.

—Carl Jung

Itinerary

We are going to explore how your core beliefs and values affect your thoughts, feelings, and behaviour; what motivates you; and the image that you project to the outside world.

Viewpoints

In this chapter, we will focus on the skills and abilities of:
- sense of purpose (keel)
- beliefs and values (hull)
- emotional awareness (rudder)
- rational thinking: deductive and inductive reasoning and questioning techniques

These have been depicted in a model of the Aurora sailing craft.

Travel Bag

You will need:
- green, blue, and red coloured pens
- journal
- collage from Chapter 1

Introduction

In this chapter, we are going to explore the essence of your being and how this impacts your outlook on life. Imagine a sailing craft that represents you, with different parts of the craft symbolising different parts of your personality. We will be looking at the part that forms the foundation and structure of who you are as a person.

I have used the keel to reflect your sense of purpose, and the hull of the boat will depict your beliefs and values. Though mostly invisible below the surface of the water, it is the keel and hull that maintain the balance of the vessel. In turn, the boat is directed by the rudder, which represents your emotions and feelings. On the whole, our emotions remain out of view, but awareness and control of them is fundamental in determining your direction and how successfully you can navigate your way through unknown waters.

Finally, the anchor represents what grounds or inhibits you in times of turbulence, insecurity and transition.

Keel: A Sense of Purpose

> The value of a man should be seen in what he gives and not in what he is able to receive.
>
> Albert Einstein

We are all unique beings and have an inimitable interpretation and perception of life and its meaning. Our life meaning is a coalescence of our cultural and religious beliefs and is mirrored by our experience of life and how we choose to interpret life events. Let's choose the keel of the craft to represent a sense of meaning. The keel is fundamental in determining the overall design and capacity of the craft. It provides the foundational supporting structure for the whole vessel.

Victor Frankl, in his book *Man's Search for Meaning*, suggests that in any situation, there are three possibilities for experiencing or creating a sense of meaning:

1. We take or learn from the experience.
2. We create or add to the experience.
3. We choose to adopt a position or attitude, no matter what the circumstances.

The Gift of Free Will

Humans have the unique ability to distance themselves from events and to see things in a broader context. The gift of free will gives us the opportunity to rise above our animal instincts and drives, to detach ourselves from our circumstances and transcend them, exhibiting our potential divine nature. Humans have the capacity to choose their attitude, emotions and behaviour, no matter what the situation. We can either be animalistic, self-seeking, and self-preserving, or we can adopt a more loving and accepting attitude. If we are given only the option to suffer, we can choose to do so with dignity.

This perfection of attitude has been attained by many of the great leaders—for example, Gandhi and Nelson Mandela. Despite the circumstances, they chose to tolerate their situation with grace and dignity. The essence of what you find to be meaningful in life is reflected in your beliefs and values.

☸ *2.1 Activity: Interpret Your Collage*

Study your collage and consider what elements of your life currently give you a sense of purpose or meaning. Record your responses to the following questions in your journal:

- Where are you *giving* and where are you *receiving*?
- What is your attitude?

Hull: Your Beliefs and Values

Beliefs are unconsciously assimilated—from the moment we are born to the day we die—from the significant people in our lives. This is particularly so during the first five years of life. These beliefs are generally reflective of the culture we are born into, and such cultural values are reinforced as we grow.

Beliefs are often adopted unconsciously and are typically ethnocentric: they are seen as the only way of doing things and should always hold true. They tend to remain unexamined and occur at an unconscious level. Our beliefs are reflected in our patterns of behaviour; style of dress; assumed roles of males and females in the family, and of youth and the elderly; language; manners; economic and class relationships; ways of coping with silence; and personal space. In fact, our beliefs affect every element of our existence.

Global Beliefs and Values

In most modern countries, the independence and self-sufficiency of a child is strongly developed and actively encouraged by parents because it is seen to be a positive quality. However, in more traditional cultures, the emphasis is placed on the family and the extended family, with the needs of the group being put before those of the individual. In these cultures, children are encouraged to be focused on their families—particularly the older generation, who will make important life decisions on their behalf. For example, the family will have a strong influence on the individual's choice of career or marriage partner. True conflict is experienced when younger generations, particularly those who have emigrated from a group-focused culture to an individual-focused culture, adopt an independent or Western approach.

Beliefs from cultures in different parts of the world vary widely along a vast spectrum of what is accepted as the norm. Obviously, within these cultures individuals exist on every point in that spectrum, but there is an overall cultural tendency to fall toward one extreme rather than the other, as demonstrated by the following stories.

A friend was living in Hong Kong and teaching English to young Chinese children. They made excellent progress, but she was frustrated in her attempts to teach them to say "thank you" to her and her assistant. They simply refused to say it. She tried hard to instil the ethic of thanking people. In frustration, after a year of trying, she asked her Chinese assistant why they refused to say thank you. Her assistant politely explained that in the Chinese culture, children are taught that they are in incredible debt to those senior to them, especially their teachers. The debt is so large that it would be an insult to express their gratitude in mere words. This new insight was extremely humbling for my friend.

The other story is a sad one about a grandfather who immigrated with his family from Russia to the United States. The grandfather committed suicide after his grandson bought a car without asking him. From the grandfather's perspective, he no longer had a role in the family and therefore his life was without meaning, while the grandson had not even thought of mentioning the prospective purchase to his grandfather.

Both these stories highlight that there are different ways of perceiving the same reality. The more you are aware of these different perspectives, the greater your level of understanding of different people, cultures, and creeds.

The beliefs and values listed in the Global Belief and Value Scale, as seen in the next activity, are selected from different cultures including Australian, American, Japanese, English, German, and Egyptian.

2.2 Activity: Find Your Point on the *Global Belief and Value Scale*

Using a green coloured pen, plot your position on the Global Belief and Value Scale that lists different cultural beliefs. Consider where you fall on each continuum and circle the point that reflects most closely your v+iew of life. For example, if you believe that your life is completely in your own hands—that is, self-determined—you would circle the * nearest that belief. Then answer the questions at the end of the activity in your journal.

Global Belief and Value Scale

Fatalism (lack of control)	*	*	*	Self-determination
Change is positive	*	*	*	Change is negative
Equality of all people	*	*	*	Privilege/status for some
Individual focus	*	*	*	Family focus
Independence/autonomy	*	*	*	Dependence on family
Personal goals valued	*	*	*	Group goals valued
Formality	*	*	*	Informality
Man separate from nature	*	*	*	Man part of nature
Materialism important	*	*	*	Spirituality important

Time moves fast	*	*	*	Time moves slowly
Sufficient resources for all	*	*	*	Resources limited
Motivation by achievement	*	*	*	Motivation for power
Competitive	*	*	*	Team approach
Intrinsic motivation	*	*	*	Extrinsic motivation
Emphasis on privacy	*	*	*	Emphasis on openness
Ethnocentrism	*	*	*	Multicultural
Conservative	*	*	*	Explorative
Supportive	*	*	*	Critical
Trusting	*	*	*	Shrewd
Equality for both sexes	*	*	*	Dominance of one sex
One supreme religion	*	*	*	All religions respected
Education and knowledge	*	*	*	Experience is superior
Democratic system	*	*	*	Tribal/chieftain system

2.3 Activity: Questions to Reflect On in Your Journal

Answer the following questions in your journal:

- To what extent did you find it easy to place yourself on the continuum and to what degree are you in line with the norms of your environment?
- Do you know of people at the other ends of the spectrum from you? Why do they think and believe as they do? What is your attitude to these people and how does that make you feel?
- Are these people from minority countries, cultures, or nationalities?
- How does this reflect your global political and social understanding?
- Have you really and truly questioned these beliefs and claimed them as your own?

2.4 Activity: Plot Your Parents' Position on the Scale

Using different coloured pens—blue and red—now plot your parents' beliefs on the Global Belief and Value Scale above. Reconsider your cultural belief assessment. Write your thoughts in your journal.

- How different are your beliefs and values from your parents'?
- How do you feel about your core beliefs and values being different from or the same as theirs?

2.5 Activity: Reflection

> Take a few moments to pause and reflect on what you have discovered so far on your journey of self-discovery. Record your thoughts and feelings in your journal.

What we believe largely determines how we perceive the world, what social and environmental cues we look out for, and how we choose to interpret these cues. With the interpretation comes our behaviour, which for a large portion of our lives has the potential to be mainly reactive. However, the more conscious of our beliefs and thoughts we become, the more we are able to consciously choose our emotional and thinking responses—and ultimately, our behaviour. This conscious awareness allows us the freedom to be happy no matter what the circumstances, as we have the free will to choose our state of mind.

When Your Beliefs Change to Values

Beliefs become values when they are rationally examined, actively and consciously chosen from a number of researched alternative beliefs, and then acted upon. The more they are integrated into your lifestyle and publicly affirmed, the more substance they have at a conscious level. Acknowledging that different beliefs can have equal meaning for different people allows you to accept that other people can choose different beliefs and values. It is their right to do so, provided it does not encroach on the rights of other people. Acceptance of other people's viewpoints is incredibly liberating, allowing for a great release of energy that is alternatively engaged in trying to convert and control others. This acknowledgement and respect for other perspectives has an important impact on all levels of your communication, leadership, and interpersonal skills.

Your beliefs and values affect your attitude toward life. The higher the level of examination of your beliefs, the higher your level of consciousness and the more you are able to choose your attitude and, ultimately, your behaviour. We will explore your values as reflected in your view of significant people in your life.

Personal Constructs

Psychologist George Kelly suggested that our view of the world can be understood by people we associate with and how we view their personal constructs (Fransella, Bell, and Bannister 2004). Our values and beliefs reflect the meaning that we give to our experience with different people and the constructs, good or bad, that we associate with them.

In the activity below, you will explore your unique constructs, which inherently reflect your values and beliefs.

2.6 Activity: Explore Your Personal Unique Constructs

Step 1: Take a piece of A4 paper and cut it into at least eighteen small squares, approximately 4x4 centimetres each. For each category listed below, select three people who fit the categories below and put their names on three of the paper squares (one name per slip of paper). *Please note, you cannot use the same person twice in the entire activity.* You will end up with eighteen slips of paper with one name on each. The categories are:

- family members that you do like
- family members that you don't like
- people that you know well and like
- people that you know well and don't like
- public people (alive or dead) that you respect and admire
- public people (alive or dead) that you don't respect or admire

Step 2: Turn over the slips of paper so that you cannot see the names written on them, mix them up, and spread them out. Now, randomly select three slips and consider the names of the people you have selected. From the three selected, choose the two that have the most personality traits in common, returning the remaining one to the original group, face down. Reflect on the two people whose names you have chosen and write a list in your journal of their common traits and characteristics, for example:

- honest
- open
- reserved
- polite
- rude
- impatient

Note: Only one trait per line.

Step 3: Once you have listed the personal constructs that these two people have in common, put the names aside and repeat Step 2 with another three slips. You do not need to rewrite the personality traits that you have already listed. Continue until you have applied the process to all the people who are listed on the slips of paper. At this point, you may choose to look at all the names and consciously choose two similar people who have characteristics you have not yet listed and add them to the list.

Step 4: When you feel that you have exhausted the process, return to the top of the list in your journal and write down what you consider to be the opposite to the characteristic listed, as shown below.

Honest	_____	Dishonest
Open	_____	Withdrawn
Reserved	_____	Outgoing
Polite	_____	Awkward
Rude	_____	Respectful
Impatient	_____	Patient

Step 5: Once you have completed this, plot along the continuum where you would position yourself and significant others in your life. Reflect in your journal any insights that you may have gained by doing this activity. Choose three personal constructs that you would like to work on during this course and consider how you might achieve this.

Rudder: Your Emotional Awareness

I have selected the craft's rudder as representing emotions and feelings. The rudder is attached to the keel and the hull of the boat and is controlled by the helm. Although relatively small, the rudder is fundamental in determining the direction in which a craft sails; if it is left unattended, havoc could result. The vessel would be vulnerable to the prevailing elements, either the winds or the currents or both. The craft would also be susceptible to the hazards of passing ships, reefs or rocky outcrops.

In essence, the rudder is fundamental not only to the successful steering of the craft but also to its very survival. In the same way, when our emotions and feelings are in turmoil and we feel unsatisfied and unhealthy, we will not be able to steer our way with clarity through life's hurdles.

Accessing and Understanding Feelings

Our emotional record is largely absorbed unconsciously and is mainly formulated in the early years of life. This record develops from the experiences that we have with our parents and prominent caregivers and how we encounter our environment. Our natural emotional disposition is determined during the first five years of our lives, at a time when we do not have a comprehensive language with which to identify feelings and emotions. During these early years, we experience a vast range of feelings and emotions, both positive and negative. The positive feelings include loving and being loved, security, playfulness, joy, creativity, and spontaneity, while the negative feelings include discomfort, feeling unloved, fear, anger, hate, greed, insecurity, isolation, and rejection.

These feelings are experienced unconsciously and if the negative emotions remain unexplored they can replay throughout our lives, with the potential of allowing us to stray dangerously off course. We also may experience times when our emotions are in neutral. Examples are when we are engaged in rational thought and are asking questions like why, what, when, how, what if, which, and so on, or when we are focused on a particular task.

Accessing these feelings and bringing them to a conscious level is made difficult by the three main factors outlined below.

1. Initial emotions are recorded during the first five years of life.

This is a time when we do not have the language and vocabulary or the cognitive ability to identify, label and record them in a systematic manner. This makes accessing them and understanding them difficult. If only we were able to reconfigure our memory system, as it is possible to do with personal computers! By understanding the source of our negative recordings, we have the possibility of reframing them in a rational, positive, and meaningful manner.

For example, an adult may experience anxiety when crossing a road. This emotion may have been registered long ago when, as a child, the person tried to cross a busy road alone and his or her mother reacted in extreme anger. The anxiety the child felt at that time may remain and be reactivated every time the (now) adult crosses a road.

As adults, if we understand the association and can rationalise the emotion as inappropriate, with time, it will stop being re-enacted. In our example, the adult would understand that the mother's reaction, although perceived and experienced as unloving and anxiety-provoking at the time, was actually based on real love and concern for the physical safety of her child. The mature and conscious adult would focus on the caring and loving intention, and in time the anxiety associated with crossing the road would diminish.

Our survival instincts often dictate our behaviour without us understanding their source and potential consequences. In our evolution as a species, the brain evolved in stages:

- The *brainstem* or *reptilian part* of the brain was the first to evolve and is concerned with the autonomic functions like blood pressure, heart rate, body temperature, breathing, and the body's basic physiological needs. It is the seat of the fight-or-flight response when we instinctively feel in danger.
- The *amygdala*, at the base of the brain stem, is concerned with our emotional response to factors both internal and external to the body.
- Emotional instinctive behaviours and reactivity are housed in the *limbic cortex*. The limbic cortex records our emotions and our long-term memories.
- The rational part of the brain is made up of the *cortex, neocortex* and *prefrontal cortex*, and developed last in man's evolutionary process. This is the thinking part of the brain and the only part that is "conscious." Language, planning, reasoning, abstract thought and working memory occur in this part of the brain.

Note that only the cortex, neocortex and prefrontal cortex have the capacity to inform the limbic system and make us conscious of our emotions. The remainder of the brain serves its amazing functions on a subconscious level. Most of our neurological pathways are from the brainstem upward. It takes conscious effort to explore and develop the pathways from the cortex, neocortex and prefrontal cortex to the limbic system so we can better understand our emotions and automatic responses.

2. We respond according to how we process information.

If we act and behave solely on the impulses received initially, we react instinctively. We use only the primitive part of our brain. The consequences are often equally as primitive. We can respond with our emotions and consequently act and think irrationally. On the other hand, if we discipline ourselves to utilise our more evolved and higher brain—the cortex and neocortex—we can think rationally and consciously choose our emotions and behaviours.

Sometimes, awareness of the source of your feelings may challenge you or be very painful. It may be easier to deny and suppress them or, alternatively and quite commonly, project them onto others. Check yourself the next time someone else's behaviour irritates you. Look carefully within yourself for elements of the same behaviour, overt or supressed.

3. Emotions determine behaviour and behaviour affects emotions.

Our emotions determine our behaviour, but equally our behaviour affects our emotions. For example, take a child who is angry. His shoulders will be hunched, arms crossed, face pouting and pointing down. If you gently and lovingly tilt his chin upward, his shoulders are forced to relax, his arms unfold, and the whole mood of the child has to change. Equally, if you force your own behaviour to reflect a positive mood or feeling, you will find a shift in your mood—perhaps not completely at first, but you will start to move to a more positive position. However, if you reinforce your feelings with negative behaviour and body language, the chances of your mood changing from negative to positive are slim.

By being more in touch with our emotions, we have the capacity to choose how we are going to allow ourselves to feel and experience the world around us. We can let old negative emotions dominate, or we can recognise them for what they are and from where they come and decide they are inappropriate to the situation. Then we can choose alternative, more appropriate positive emotions.

Even if your emotions are appropriate to the situation, you can choose to acknowledge them but not remain with them. Viktor Frankl (1970) explains that even in the most adverse circumstances of the concentration camps during the Second World War, some prisoners were able to rise above their situation and feel compassion and love for their fellow prisoners instead of hate and anger toward their captors. By becoming aware of our emotions and taking responsibility for them, we can start to understand ourselves and others better, managing and choosing our emotions more effectively. This enlightenment requires consciously increasing the gap between what you feel, how you think, and how you behave. Below is a very simplified drawing of the brain and its cortical (conscious) and subcortical (subconscious) functioning.

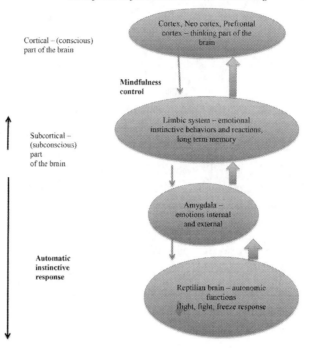

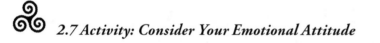

2.7 Activity: Consider Your Emotional Attitude

In the following exercise, pause and consider what your typical behaviours, thoughts, and feelings are, on the various dimensions of your life as listed below. Make notes on each in your journal. For example:

- life dimension: The clothes that I wear
- behaviour: I wear clothes that are baggy and easy to wash and wear.
- think: I think they are practical and hide the extra kilos I've put on!
- feel: I feel comfortable, but not very smart!

Life Dimensions

- the clothes that I wear
- my financial position and interests
- my eating habits
- my occupation
- my level of fitness
- my sexual orientation
- my leisure activities
- my spiritual/religious outlook
- my core family involvement

- my extended family involvement
- my friends
- my personal growth activities
- my approach to death and dying
- my personality strengths
- my personality weaknesses

2.8 Activity: Reflection

Remember, we have the capacity to choose how we feel at any given time. It is this quality that makes us potentially superior to other animals. Think about how you can raise your level of positive emotions and therefore your sense of self-worth and self-attunement. Make a note of your thoughts and what you are going to do in your journal.

What anchors you and keeps you safe in times of struggle and uncertainty? There are individual people and organisations than can support and nurture us in times of need, until the storm has passed. They provide stability when we are being battered by the elements or our own internal turmoil. For example, it may be a family member, a special friend, a counsellor, a support group, or a religious organisation. Do you consciously nurture and maintain these relationships so that they are accessible when you need them?

As Stephen Covey suggests in his book *The 7 Habits of Highly Effective People*, we have to have made emotional deposits in order to later make withdrawals from our relationships' emotional bank accounts.

2.9 Activity: Reflection

Who are the significant people in your life, how do they anchor you, and who are you an anchor for and how?

Craig Ballantyne

CHAPTER 3

Designing and Building Your Sailing Craft: Above the Water Line

The real voyage of discovery consists not in seeking new landscapes but in having new eyes.

—Marcel Proust

Itinerary

Using the sailing-craft analogy, we will look at the helm, mast, sails, crow's nest, cargo, ensign, figurehead, and compass as viewpoints. We are going to explore how your core beliefs and values affect your thoughts, feelings, and behaviour; what motivates you; and the image you project to the world.

Viewpoints

In this chapter, we will focus on:
- rational thinking—deductive and inductive reasoning (helm)
- self-esteem (mast)
- motivation (sails)
- sense of vision (crow's nest)
- image of identity (figurehead)
- sense of self (ensign)
- creativity (design your own craft)
- resources (treasures and burdens)
- ethical guide (compass)

Travel bag

You will need:
- green, blue, and red coloured pencils and pens
- journal
- collage from Chapter 1
- materials to draw your own craft
- daily diary
- access to the Internet

Introduction

In this chapter, you will be given an opportunity to creatively develop your own craft. The upper part of your sailing craft is more visible to the world around you but will be determined largely by your supporting structure. Cognisance and understanding of your beliefs, values and the emotions that you attach to them is achieved through rational analysis and thought.

The *helm* of the craft represents this rational questioning ability. It allows you, the captain, to understand yourself and the external circumstances in which you find yourself—for example, the current and the prevailing winds.

The *mast* depicts the amalgamation of these factors, your level of self-esteem. The *crow's nest* is housed on the mast, and so it follows that the level of your self-esteem determines the extent and accuracy of how you view yourself, your surroundings, and the role you play. Therefore, the crow's nest reflects your degree of vision. The *sails* will be used to reflect your life-motivating characteristics.

The *cargo* reflects what you are carrying, your resources, and the extent to which these may or may not be of value to you. The *ensign* is your attitude, sense of responsibility, and initiative; the *figurehead* reflects your sense of identity; and the *compass* reflects your moral code.

Helm: Your Rational Thinking

The helm reflects your rational scientific-inquiry ability. It represents the Einstein that is in all of us, the Socratic questions—what, where, why, how, which, when, and where—that we ask when trying to understand a situation or a problem. The content and exercises that you have tackled so far have encouraged you to use your rational inductive and deductive reasoning powers. Although it is often monotonous and laborious to examine the elements of a situation in fine detail, it is only when this is done and the information is understood within the broader picture that a true and deeper understanding can be achieved.

Rational behaviour is determined by rational thinking—the scientific enquiry into the unique personal facets of a situation. It occurs in the neocortex portion of the brain. By understanding your emotions, you free up space to allow for more positive and rational feelings to become part of your natural disposition. This, in turn, affects your automatic responses. The key is in allowing yourself time to consider your feelings and the situation before you react and act.

We do not just drift into a position of deeper understanding but rather arrive there after making a conscious decision to do so and then by continually working at it. Rational thought is preceded by exploring a situation, thought, or emotion and asking questions. Rational thought is achieved through asking these questions of yourself, your environment and those around you, repeatedly.

Once you've established the parameters of a situation, you are better able to chart your course successfully with a minimum of stress and risk. There are times in our lives, as there are with sailing, when the circumstances are beyond our control. Imagine being out on the ocean when a raging storm is imminent. You may choose to find a safe sanctuary and drop anchor or, alternatively, protect yourself, batten down the hatches, and ride out the storm until it is over.

Craig Ballantyne

When you next feel overwhelmed by an emotion, ask yourself, what is the deeper underlying root of this emotion? Is this emotion appropriate to your current situation, or is it reflective of the vulnerable child within or a set of beliefs that you no longer hold to be true? As the mature person you now are, you are capable of understanding your emotion and its source and choosing another way of thinking and behaving—and, with time, feeling.

Through rational examination, we become aware of our beliefs, values and feelings, and with time this awareness allows us to actively choose our emotional response to other people and situations. With this comes a sense of control and meaning, which resonates through our behaviour.

Rational examination of beliefs can be presented as an equation:

Unexamined beliefs and attitudes　　　+　　　Reactive behaviour
　　　　　　　　　　　　　　　　　　= An undiscerning/reactive behaviour

whereas

Examined beliefs　　+　　Emotional awareness
　　　　　　　　　　　= Self-determined meaningful behaviour

Positively managing your feelings frees up an enormous amount of energy. The positive feeling of self-control enhances your health and general feeling of self-esteem.

Mast: Your Self-Esteem

In Chapter 2, you were introduced to the analogy of a sailing craft's hull to depict your beliefs and values. In Chapter 3, we now explore the mast, which is supported by the hull and which has been selected as the symbol to reflect your level of self-esteem.

Self-esteem is defined as the composite result of your beliefs, perceptions, opinions, and attitude toward yourself—how worthy you see yourself as being. Self-esteem is developed through a process of experience with the outside world and is mainly consolidated during the first five years of life. It is either nurtured or stunted according to the person's experiences and interrelationships, particularly with parents and caregivers. The hull and the keel support the mast, and its stability and strength is determined by how cohesively and coherently the timbers—that is, your values and beliefs—are reflected by your lifestyle. These personal beliefs can be revisited at any time in your life and, with concerted effort, can be remodelled.

How Your Self-Opinions Affect How You Behave

A person's level of self-esteem affects his or her expectation of success or failure. This perception is often the precursor, more than any other factor, of the outcome. People who believe they are popular, clever, and successful will act quite different from people who see themselves as unpopular and unsuccessful. Individuals with a low level of self-esteem are often self-conscious and easily embarrassed. They tend to be shy, timid, unsure, and reserved when tackling a new situation or meeting a new person. They are likely to be inhibited and are prone to suffering from anxiety and depression.

On the other hand, those with a high level of self-esteem tend to be more self-confident, self-assured, poised, and self-reliant. They are positive and able to make decisions in an assertive and decisive manner. They have a high level of self-respect. They are more likely to be tenacious and to achieve the goals they set for themselves.

Once the level of self-esteem is set, it is not easily amended. New information that is consistent with one's own expectations is easily assimilated and absorbed, but experiences that indicate a contrary perception are difficult to adopt. This is particularly so for beliefs and values held closely to the person's inner core, to their keel. In building and maintaining your craft, you need to focus on positive core beliefs rather than negative ones.

One has to consciously challenge negative beliefs about oneself and strongly focus on a positive self-perception. Enhancing one's self-esteem is possible through consciously and carefully creating a safe, stable, predictable, and secure environment where one can nurture oneself. For example, plan for success by dividing your goals into a number of small and easily achievable steps. Give yourself small challenges that are achievable and where there is a high chance of success. Encourage yourself to try new activities and experiences without fear of failure. Put yourself in situations where you have freedom of choice and freedom to make mistakes.

How to View Failure

It is best to view failure simply as an opportunity to learn. When things don't work out as planned, try the following strategies:

- Look for the funny side and don't take the result personally.
- Surround yourself with positive and supportive people who praise, facilitate and support your successes.
- Choose friends who are warm, calm and accepting.
- Try to find a mentor who will positively affirm you and actively develop you.
- Remember, people who try to dominate and threaten, or who are sarcastic, tend to rob or lower one's self-esteem.

3.1 Activity: Complete an Online Character Strength Profile

It is important to be conscious of, draw on, and celebrate your strengths. Complete the online VIA Inventory of Strengths Survey at http://viacharacter.org/www/ and reflect on your findings in your journal.

- Were there any surprises—that is, strengths, you found out about by doing this activity? Were they pleasant ones?
- How will your character strengths help you on your journey of self-discovery?
- Do you have any weaknesses? If so, what are they and were you aware of them before?

How could they impact on your journey of self-discovery?

There are consequences to not being true to our beliefs and values. Keeping in mind the sailing-craft analogy, when we are not true to or fail to maintain our values and beliefs in the way we live our lives, we have the potential of taking in water. Our self-esteem is lowered, and in the worst-case scenario, this can cause us to sink. Consider for a moment how you view your beliefs and values. Are they positive or negative? Are your beliefs and values reflected by your lifestyle?

We will now do an activity where you will sketch a hull and write on it your sense of purpose, beliefs and values, and your attitude and perception toward each one. You will then see how closely (or not) your lifestyle reflects your beliefs and values.

3.2 Activity: Determine Your Level of Self-Esteem

Step 1: Spend a moment looking at the sailing craft on the following page. Look at the hull and then sketch your own hull in your journal. Draw it as large as you can and add into it as many segments as you can.

Step 2: Label beliefs and values, including those you are currently not putting into practice. The keel reflects what gives you a sense of meaning, what it is that gets you out of bed in the morning.

Craig Ballantyne

Step 3: Now, colour in your segments. Use green for those beliefs and values that are currently reflected in your life and red for those you're not reflecting in your current lifestyle.

Step 4: Now look at your craft and assess how congruent your lifestyle is with your beliefs. Are you surprised? Answer the following questions in your journal:

- What does your hull reflect?
- How congruent is your behaviour with your belief system?
- How well integrated is your hull?

Each red segment is potentially damaging to your self-esteem. How can you positively address these potentially damaging opinions? How could this be achieved? Give yourself a percentage estimate to the extent that your lifestyle reflects what you believe and value. What have you learnt from this exercise?

The mast is housed in the hull. The more congruent your hull—your values and beliefs—is with your lifestyle, the stronger and higher your level of self-esteem. Positively building your self-esteem has an exponential beneficial effect. In time, with care, it will develop a momentum of its own. A self-esteem questionnaire is available at http://www.wwnorton.com/college/psych/psychsci/media/rosenberg.htm.

Consider the sailing craft analogy. You know that the mast supports the crow's nest and sails, your potential for vision and motivation. Keep in mind that the greater the height of the mast, the higher your level of self-awareness and cohesion and the more you are able to be self-directed and see and monitor your course to a predetermined destination. Think about how cohesive you are, how in tune you are, how much your values and beliefs are reflected in your lifestyle.

Your level of self-esteem is fundamental to your whole outlook on life. Raising it requires integrating your beliefs and values, positively harnessing your emotions through rational thinking, and acting congruently by directing your behaviour to appropriate attainable goals. Unfortunately, a low level of self-esteem reflects a shortened mast, leaving us with a limited view of the world around us and a tendency to be self-focused and to take events personally.

Craig Ballantyne

Sails Unfurled: Your Motivating Factors

In considering what motivates us, I have included a number of differing motivational theories; the sails reflect theories including those by Maslow (1954), Frankl (1970), and McClelland (2000). Maslow's motivational element has been used to determine the vertical capacity of the sail (see illustration).

The foundation of Maslow's hierarchy of needs is the pursuit of physical extrinsic needs primary to our survival, such as food, housing and security. The carnal animal nature is reflected in our basic needs of survival, territory and power. Maslow suggests that once the most primitive of our survival needs are met, we have the choice to move to the satisfaction of higher order needs, such as social acceptance, self-esteem and finally self-actualisation. I would like to add the concept of enlightenment to the pinnacle of the pyramid. Enlightenment can be defined as the reflection of the image of God or the spark of goodness that is within us all.

An excessive desire and striving for external material items (extrinsic needs) may cause us to benchmark our sense of self-esteem and of meaning against attaining material items. It also means our sense of self-worth is at the mercy of others. Intrinsic or internal levels of satisfaction and meaning simply require our own input and chosen perception.

Frankl was interned in one of the concentration camps during the Second World War. He closely studied how some people interned under the most hideous of circumstances managed to maintain a sense of self-worth and dignity and were able to subsequently build a new life at the end of the war. He suggests that in any situation, we can be motivated by what we receive or gain from it, what we give to it, or a combination of both. This element determines the horizontal capacity we have to unfurl the sails. Our sail unravels from the centre, to both the left and the right. Unfurling from the mast on the left is the extent to which we are motivated by giving, and unfurling from the right by receiving.

> Everything can be taken from a man but one thing, the last of the human freedoms: to choose one's attitude in any given set of circumstances, to choose one's own way (Frankl 1970, 45).

Contrary to Maslow, Frankl believes that we can satisfy the higher-order needs of self-actualisation and enlightenment without the lower-order needs being met. Through our free will, we can choose our attitude; despite our circumstances, we can create a feeling of unconditional love. I have combined these differing theories and demonstrate them diagrammatically below.

Types of Motivators

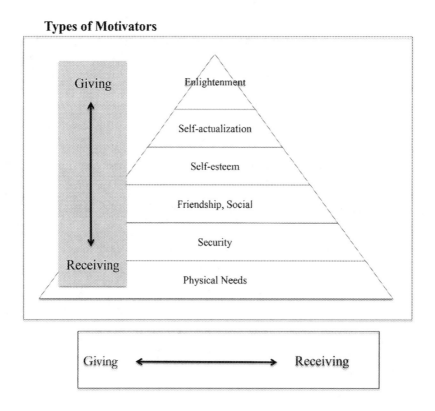

McClelland suggests that people tend to be *achievement-orientated*, *affiliate-orientated* or *power-orientated* in their motivation. Achievers tend to be task-orientated and like regular feedback on their progress. They like to work alone or with other achievers. Affiliators, on the other hand, seek harmonious relationships with other people and like to feel they are a part of a team. Power people like to direct and control others.

Motivation is a complex factor in determining how we respond and emotionally react to a situation or another person. It is in better understanding what motivates ourselves and others that we can guide and take control of our circumstances and behaviour.

3.3 Activity: Review Your Daily Diary for Motivation Levels

Step 1: Complete a daily diary of all of your activities for one week.

Step 2: Review your daily entries and consider your level of motivation in terms of the theories outlined above. Re-examine your daily diary entries over the last week or longer. Consider your level of motivation in three of the entries and make a note of when you are giving and when you are receiving. Now, colour these instances green if you were happy, content and fulfilled; blue if you were feeling neutral; and red if you are feeling angry, depressed, annoyed, or otherwise negative.

Step 3: Review your daily entries and list the hierarchy of needs. Revisit your diary and indicate on it which of your hierarchy of needs you are satisfying for each segment of time. Use the key below:

P physical needs
S security
F friendship, social
SE self-esteem
SA self-actualisation
E enlightenment

Step 4: In your journal, answer the following questions:

- From your daily diary, what percentage of time (roughly) did you spend in each motivational state?
- Is this a true reflection of your motivational life?
- What are the internal and external factors that contribute to this disposition?
- How do these affect you?
- To what extent do these motivations have their roots in childhood experiences?
- Is there a particular time or place when you are more susceptible to certain moods than others? List them.
- Any other things that you have noticed?
- Are your motivators intrinsic or extrinsic? Explain.
- What activities would you like to be doing more, and which ones less?
- In an ideal world, how would you like to be spending your time?

Note that there is no perfectly shaped sail. Each of us is different, with different motivational needs that vary from day to day, and situation to situation, just as the degree and angle to which a sail is unfurled is dependent on the environment, weather conditions and the intended destination, at a certain point on time.

Crow's Nest: Your Degree of Vision

The crow's nest allows you, the captain, the opportunity to observe what is happening below on the deck as well as further out to sea. This analogy can be taken a step further to include the height of the mast bearing the crow's nest as reflective of our self-esteem. We find that the lower the self-esteem, the closer we are to the deck.

Individuals with a crow's nest close to the deck have a tendency to be self-absorbed and self-centred. They are apt to take things extremely personally. Regrettably, because they have such a limited peripheral view, they also tend to be negative in their outlook. They can be inclined to feel threatened easily and become defensive quickly. They often lack insight into their feelings and are not open to receiving ideas that differ from their own. They have a tendency to withdraw and become submissive for fear of angering others, or alternatively, they go on the attack at the slightest perceived provocation.

The consequence of this is that our peripheral view of the deck and the surrounding area is reduced. In the extreme case, if we have no self-esteem, we find ourselves at the level of the deck, with no peripheral view at all! Alternatively, if we have a high level of self-esteem and an elevated crow's nest, we are able to see far and wide. Furthermore, we can see our craft in correct relation to the context and the environment in which we find ourselves. Our outlook is more realistic and dependable, and we have sight of potential hazards up ahead. This enhanced view and insight allows us time to anticipate and take appropriate corrective action to avoid potential crises and hazards.

 3.4 Activity: Reflection

Reflect on your level of self-esteem by revisiting your journal. Similarly, look again at your sketch of the hull you did in Activity 3.2. Give yourself a rough estimate of the level of your self-esteem. Consider the following questions and then make a note of your reflections and insights in your journal:

- What did you find when revisiting your journal and the beliefs and values of your hull?
- How close are you to the deck? Another way of considering this is how self-absorbed are you currently? Or are you near the heavens with an expanded outlook on life and your role in it?
- What are the factors that you need to revisit to improve your self-esteem and outlook?

You will be given the opportunity to revisit your emotional awareness in further legs of your journey.

Cargo: Your Treasures and/or Burdens

Take a moment to reflect on what resources or cargo you are taking on your journey of self-discovery and personal development. Consider if there is any unnecessary cargo you may be carrying. What old hurts and resentments are weighing you down and impeding your mobility, flexibility, and progress? How are they helpful in continuing to define who you are, or would you benefit from gently throwing them overboard?

Craig Ballantyne

Figurehead: Your Image or Identity

We all carry around with us a perception of who we are and how we fit into the world—for example, earth mother, tough up-and-coming executive, philosopher, artist. These perceptions of who we are affect many of the cues we give to the world—how we dress and eat, the friends we choose to associate with, the car we drive (or aspire to drive). To illustrate this element of our persona—the one that we aspire to project to the world—I have used the figurehead that is found on the front of old sailing ships.

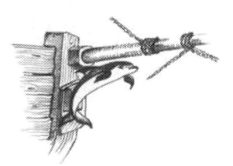

Craig Ballantyne

Think about the image that you like to reflect. Think about a symbol that stands for who you are—maybe a peace sign, a BMW logo, or an eagle. In considering the Aurora sailing craft, a dolphin was selected. A dolphin for me depicts a great zest for life, the joy of frolicking in the waves while having a strong sense of community and social responsibility, and a finely tuned intelligence and sensitivity.

Ensign: Your Attitude, Initiative, and Sense of Responsibility

The finishing touch to a sailing craft is its ensign—its flag—which may include a name or emblem. The name and flag herald your intentions to the outside world. This is your sense of responsibility. To what extent do you take ownership for who you are and the circumstances you find yourself in? The more you recognise your role, the more likely you will be to take the initiative to change yourself or the things around you.

Is your ensign a skull and crossbones, typically depicting an attitude that the world owes you a living and that anything that goes wrong is someone else's fault? Alternatively, is your ensign similar to that of the UN Peace Force flag, displaying the intention to attain world peace through active involvement? Your ensign is at the pinnacle of your craft. It reflects your attitude, initiative, and sense of responsibility. It is an integral part of who you are and how you act.

Symbolism as an Expression of Man's Values and Beliefs

Symbolism has played an important role in the expression of man's values and beliefs since prehistory. Take, for example, the symbols of concentric spirals.

The clockwise spiral, one of the world's oldest symbols, was found carved by the Cro-Magnons on a mammoth's tooth reputed to be 24,000 years old. The spiral was carved onto rocks by the ancient Scandinavians to record the eclipses of the sun. In ancient Ireland, it was used to represent the sun. The spiral appears on Neolithic rock carvings in Utah and is a symbol used to depict power in Tibet. It appears on all sorts of artefacts found in Europe dating back to the Bronze Age. In ancient Greece, it was used to decorate vases and amphorae. The Celts used the spiral to represent cosmic growth. Similarly, the Maori people call it Koru, the unfolding stem frond of a fern, a symbol of the unfolding of eternal life.

I have chosen the triskelion or triple spiral to be the ensign for the Aurora sailing craft. The craft is called Aurora, meaning *rising light,* and the three spirals support the name.

Aurora

Colours are important in ensigns. Consider how some colours are perceived:

- red—high energy, passion, vibrancy, stimulation, love, courage, strength
- blue—tranquillity, calming, healing, peace, sacredness
- yellow—intelligence, spirituality, peace, wisdom, divination, thanksgiving
- white (reflects all other colours)—purity, tenderness
- green (combination of yellow and blue)—abundance, fertility, prosperity, healing, spirituality
- orange (combination of red and yellow)—creativity, support, warmth, vibrancy, intelligence
- purple (combination of red and blue)—regality, power, royalty, wealth
- black (absorbs all other colours)—strength, negativity, hidden intentions, power
- brown (combination of yellow, red, and black)—earthliness, animality

3.5 Activity: Design Your Ensign

It is now time for you to take all the concepts introduced so far and include them in the design of your ensign. Think about what type of ensign you would like on your sailing craft. Also, think about what colour you would like it to be and what colours are representative of you and your craft.

Use your journal to design the ensign. You may find that doing some research into symbolism might be helpful. For example, you may discover other ancient symbols like the spiral that have significance for you that can also be easily incorporated. Now describe the meaning of your design.

The ensign is a composite of the values and beliefs that reflect who you are as a person. This exercise will help you to integrate your ideas and be better able to recall them later. It will also help you to make them your own.

Compass: Your Ethical Guide

There are many possible sources of compass points or references that guide us in our actions and decision-making, including religious principles or an organisation that we are affiliated with and which provides a required code of conduct. The key is in ensuring that this ethical guide is available to be used as a reference point when we feel lost and at sea with challenging situations and circumstances.

3.6 Activity: Ethical Guide

In your journal, note your guiding ethical principles and reflect on how you keep them evident in your life so they are accessible when needed.

3.7 Activity: Create Your Own Craft

Now is the opportunity for you to create your own sailing craft model from scratch. Think of a model that includes all the viewpoints mentioned, such as hull, keel, rudder, sails, helm, and so on.

Make a sketch in your journal. Imagine the type of journey you would like to take on your own voyage of self-discovery. Design and draw the type of sailing craft that would meet all of your requirements. You will be able to make improvements on it at your own discretion during the journey. Part of the beauty of an imaginary journey is that you can amend the structure whenever and however you need to. Include as much detail as you can. This practical activity is designed to challenge your creativity but also to test your inductive and deductive reasoning. Be as creative as you can and enjoy yourself.

CHAPTER 4

Plotting Your Co-ordinates - Choosing Your Destination and Planning Your Stopovers

Autobiography in Five Chapters

I walk down the street.
There is a deep hole in the sidewalk
I fall in.
I am lost … I am hopeless.
It isn't my fault.
It takes forever to find a way out.

I walk down the same street.
There is a deep hole in the sidewalk.
I pretend I don't see it.
I fall in again.
I can't believe I'm in the same place.
But it isn't my fault.
It takes a long time to get out.

I walk down the same street.
There is a deep hole in the sidewalk
I see it there.
I still fall in … it's a habit.
My eyes are open.
I know where I am.
It is my fault.
I get out immediately.

I walk down the same street.
There is a deep hole in the sidewalk.
I walk around it.
I walk down another street.

—Portia Nelson

Itinerary

In this chapter, you will learn about selecting a goal, decision analysis, task analysis, improving time utilisation, and planning to achieve your goal.

Viewpoints

We will focus on:
- deductive and inductive reasoning
- focus of attention
- goal-setting
- decision-making
- initiative
- global perspective
- vision

Travel bag

You will need
- daily diary from your Activity 3.3
- yellow and blue Post-it notes
- a calendar or daily, monthly, and annual planner
- your journal
- access to the Internet

Introduction

Well done! You have now completed extensive personal research into who you are and what you value and aspire to. In this leg of your journey, you are going to focus on goals and how to achieve the things that are important in your life. Although this chapter is a bit dry, hang in there! Be self-disciplined and apply yourself fully, and with time and practice, the thinking patterns suggested in this section will become automatic.

You will have the opportunity to explore potential life dreams and set a SMART goal (see below about SMART) to achieve one of them. The next step is to develop a detailed plan itemising the steps and decisions that you will have to make in order to achieve your dream goal. Consideration also must be given to possible constraints you need to consider and plan for. There may be alternative routes to take. Achieving your goal may not be a linear experience, and you may be able to tackle different elements of it simultaneously, speeding up the process. This requires organisation and management of your time and resources.

You will then analyse how you currently spend your time and consider how you can better allocate time to enable you to achieve your goal. Finally, you will be given the opportunity to reflect on the process of changing old personal habits. This takes time and dedicated effort.

Let us start with choosing a suitable goal and exploring possible destinations. In the three previous chapters, you have explored many different aspects of who you are and where you are at the present time. Let's explore where you would like to be in the future.

4.1 Activity: Identifying Your Life Dreams

> In your journal, record a random wish list of all the dreams that you would like to achieve in your lifetime. Don't be inhibited by wealth, time, opportunity, family commitments, or the like. Be as expansive and creative as you can. This is a chance for great ideas and dreams to be realised. Often when you write them down, they become tangible—and this is the first step toward achieving them.

Criteria for a SMART Goal

A SMART goal is a goal that is specific and measureable. It demonstrates that you know exactly what you want to achieve. SMART goals have a far greater chance of being successful than a general goal because they are detailed and identify the who, what, when, where, which, and why of your goal. SMART is an acronym for:

S: Specific
M: Measureable
A: Achievable
R: Resources/Reasonable
T: Timeline

Below is a list of criteria that should be part of a good goal. It should:

- be one that you feel you own and want to achieve
- be reflective of your beliefs and values
- have intrinsic and/or extrinsic value
- be attainable in small, measurable chunks
- be observable
- be something that you will be able to share in public
- have immediate short-term benefits
- have the potential of benefiting you and those around you
- be clearly written, concise, well-defined, and specific, with the required action, measurement criteria (before and after), and finite completion date—nothing wishy-washy!

Note the potential positive and negative consequences of achieving your goal. An example of a well-defined SMART goal is:

> In six weeks' time, I will have taken my family away for a weekend to enjoy the outdoors and have quality family time through storytelling and a family treasure hunt. The benefits will be relaxation as a family and a better appreciation of each other and the outdoors. The negative may be a withdrawal from the savings account!

In this example, the measurable criteria is a family weekend away within six weeks, with family time together measured by family storytelling and a treasure hunt using clues from the outdoors. Financial costs are included as a consideration.

4.2 Activity: Choose and Define Your Six-Week SMART Goal

In your journal, compose an easily manageable SMART goal that you can achieve during the next six weeks. Perhaps it is one of your dreams identified in Activity 4.1. Write it as specifically and as clearly as possible. Identify and note the milestones you will use in order to measure whether or not you have achieved the goal. Also record the positive and possible negative consequences you anticipate on achieving your goal. Check your goal against the criteria of a good goal as listed above.

En Route Incentives

When choosing a goal, ideally it should have its own intrinsic value to you. But this is often not the case, because en route we may have to pass certain landmarks (in navigational terms) that can mean discomfort. In these situations, you can apply incentives to the goal by promising yourself a reward on successfully passing these waypoints.

For example, I wanted to qualify as a psychologist so that I could do the work I really enjoyed and work flexible hours to accommodate a young family. This entailed attaining both an honours and a master's degree, in often theoretical, unrelated, and uninteresting topics. In order to provide some sort of incentive for myself—the prospect of flexible working hours seemed too far off (I was on a five-year study plan)—I promised myself a trip to Thailand if I attained my honours, a reasonable halfway mark. That provided the necessary incentive, and both were achieved!

4.3 Activity: List En Route Incentives

In your journal, list positive appropriate incentives and rewards that would encourage you to complete your goal and make the steps along the way less arduous.

Pareto's Principle—The 80:20 Rule

This principle applies across many situations, from sales to time spent completing an assessment. In short, the theory says that 80 per cent of the desired result is achieved in 20 per cent of the time. In order to achieve the full 100 per cent potential result, the remaining 20 per cent of the desired result requires an investment of a further 80 per cent of time and resources. So in the example of writing a training course, an 80 per cent quality result would be achieved in 20 per cent of the time required to achieve a 100 per cent result. The person developing the course is then left with the option of developing one course at a quality of 100 per cent or five courses at 80 per cent. (See the following page.)

The reality is that most people would not notice the added 20 per cent of quality, as they would have their unique way of viewing the content and would have a slightly different view, as we all see things differently. In this case, the person who has invested so much extra time in achieving their perception of 100 per cent may then be resistant to adding in the suggestions or ideas of some one else, no matter how valid. Some things are worth giving your all to and achieving the best you can, while in other cases, lots of 80 per cent quality is much better use of your time and resources. The key is being conscious of which option you are choosing to fulfil.

Pareto's Principle—The 80:20 Rule

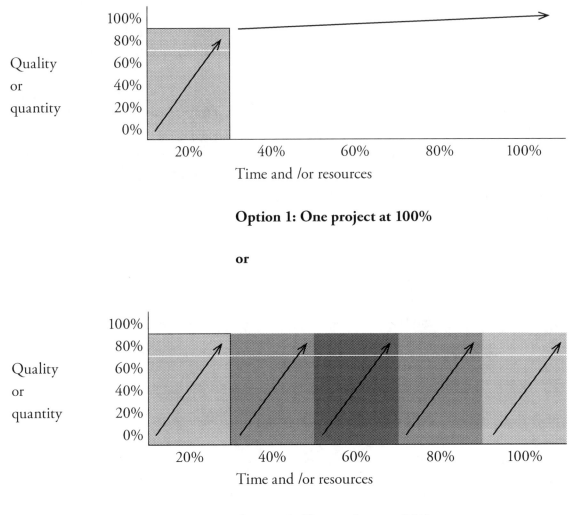

Option 1: One project at 100%

or

Option 2: Five projects at 80%

Using a Decision Matrix

Each day, we make a mountain of decisions, often unconsciously. Sometimes we procrastinate, but our inertia still precipitates a decision, even if it's a non-decision. A decision matrix can be useful when you're trying to make an important decision and there are a number of people involved, or if there are a number of options, or if there is a high degree of emotional involvement, or any combination of the above. This method allows you to fully be at the ship's helm while taking into account the personal interests of everyone involved. A decision matrix:

- evaluates and prioritises a list of options
- is logical
- involves you establishing a list of weighted criteria and then evaluating each option against those criteria

4.4 Activity: Do a Decision Analysis

Look at the example below of a family choosing which holiday destination best meets the criteria they identified when they set their "weekend away" goal. After you've looked at the example and their decision matrix, conduct your own decision matrix on a decision you have been contemplating. In your journal, reflect on what you've learnt.

The choice is between:

> *Option 1:* A family weekend at the beach for three full days, and everyone can come, except for Aunt Bessie.
>
> *Option 2:* A family weekend in the mountains for two days, and everyone can attend, including Aunt Bessie.

Steps for a decision matrix:

1. List the criteria
2. Decide how important the criteria are, on a scale of 1-10, 1 being the least important and 10 being the most important.
3. List the possible options and evaluate each option against the criteria, again using the scale of 1-10, 1 being the least important and 10 being the most important.
4. Multiply the weight of each criterion against the degree to which the option meets that criterion and record the outcome.
5. Add all the weighted scores for each option and total.
6. Compare the total outcomes of each option and determine which appears to be the best outcome.

**Example Decision Matrix:
Choosing a Holiday Destination**

1. Criteria	2. Weighting of Importance	3. Option 1: Three days – but no Aunt Bessie Degree to which it meets each criterion	4. Degree to which option meets each criterion (column 2 vs column 3)	5. Option 2: Two days—whole family Degree to which it meets each criterion	6. Degree to which option meets each criterion (column 2 vs column 5)
Family away	10	4	40	10	100
Quality time	10	10	100	10	100
Outdoors	8	10	80	10	80
Relaxing	7	10	70	10	70
Budget	4	4 (more expensive)	16	8	32
Total			306		382

From the above matrix, it becomes apparent that the second option is the better choice given all the factors involved.

Identifying and Planning to Reach Your Final Ports of Call—A Task Analysis

A task is a series of actions or activities that naturally occur together. A task analysis is a summary of all the tasks and decisions that need to be taken in order to reach your goal. Going back to our sailing-craft analogy, ports of call are the stopovers that you need to make en route to achieve your destination. In terms of the above example, on a weekend away with the family, the ports of call before going on holiday would probably include:

- family requirements and availability
- transport
- location
- family activities
- supplies

The activities associated with each of these tasks may include the following:

Family Requirements and Availability
(useful when applying the decision-making matrix when selecting the location)

- Ask family members what activities they would like to do over the weekend.
- Ask which dates they are available.
- Ask what their budget and time constraints are.
- Ask how they will be travelling there.
- Ask if there are any specific personal requirements they have for the location, such as special diet or separate bedroom for children.

Transport

- Determine transport availability.
- Think about the type of transport required.
- Fill the car with petrol.

Location

- Research possible locations.
- Assess travel time, cost, facilities, availability, and so on.
- Regard preferences of family members.

Family activities

- Pack some family games.
- Pack some photo albums and family videos to look at while away.
- Verify if the accommodation has a TV/video facility.
- Buy a new game to play.
- Gather items/ideas for the treasure hunt.
- Pack the clothes.
- Pack the car.

Supplies

- Determine budget.
- Research restaurants.

- Discuss and plan menu.
- Do the grocery shopping.

4.5 Activity: Plot Your Ports of Call—A Task Analysis

In this activity, you are going to plot your ports of call to help you achieve the goal you wrote in Activity 4.2.

Step 1: List all the tasks needed to reach your goal. Revisit your goal from Activity 4.2. Then, in your journal, brainstorm and randomly list all the tasks you will have to achieve in order to reach your goal—your destination.

Step 2: List all the activities that relate to each task. There may be some confusion over which is a task and which is an activity. Do not concern yourself with this—what is important is that you list everything that needs to be done in order to achieve your end goal, either as a task or as an activity.

Step 3: Decide on the critical decision points that must be considered so that you can achieve your goal. Write these down in your journal.

Step 4: Group the activities into tasks. Put each task onto its own yellow Post-it note. List all the activities related to the task on blue Post-it notes. Now group your activities under the appropriate task. Once you have completed your list of tasks, look again at your goal and ask yourself whether, if you achieve all these steps/tasks, you will have fulfilled all the elements of your goal or destination. If not, revisit your to-do list and your planned steps until you are satisfied you have covered your entire goal criterion.

Be aware of *nice to haves*. Prune your plan to include only what is relevant and essential to achieving your goal. Many a goal goes unachieved by being lost in a maze of activities. Note what decisions will need to be made as part of the process. In prioritising your planning, consider which step is an unconditional prerequisite to another, and place it below that step. Place tasks that can occur simultaneously alongside or parallel to each other.

Example of a Task Analysis

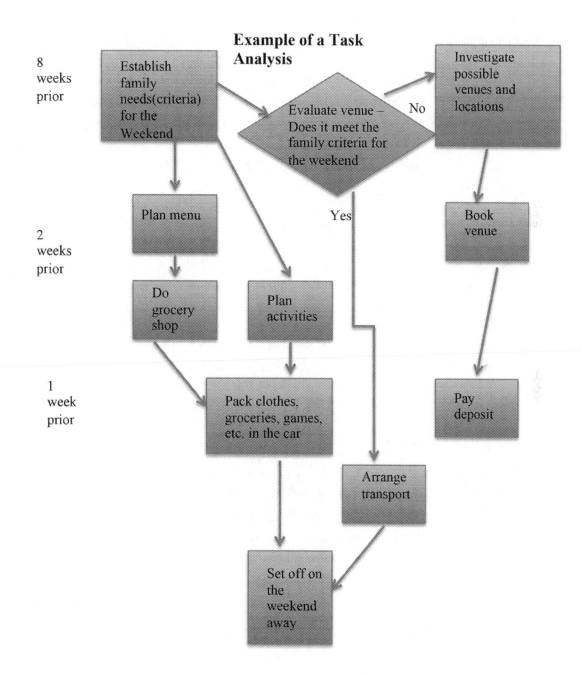

8 weeks prior

2 weeks prior

1 week prior

The Weather Forecast for the Period

It is now time to be Machiavellian in our approach. In the sixteenth century, Machiavelli wrote an excellent little book for the reigning Italian Crown Prince on how to manage his resources and generally outwit his opponents. All the principles he promoted are just as applicable today. Machiavelli recommended that when facing a potential conflict with an adversary, it is best to plan ahead and engage at a time of your choice. If you allow your opponent to choose the time, it is likely to be when you are at a greater disadvantage.

Consider the elements and individuals that may pose constraints on you achieving your goal, such as budget and time; lack of support from family and friends; and limited skills, capacity, or facilities. Think of ways you can initiate support and address potential constraints positively and proactively. What are the things you can do and say to prevent these constraints from even occurring? By being proactive in addressing problems in a timely way, you will minimise unnecessary conflict. Think about those around you:

- How could they be party to you reaching your goal?
- What are their personal goals and ambitions?
- What are their values?
- What are the likely elements that you could include in your exercise that would mutually benefit all parties involved?

You will be amazed at how alternative options become possible once you are open to the idea that there can be mutual benefits for all those involved.

4.6 Activity: Identify and Plan for Potential Constraints

Think about potential constraints to achieving your goal. This entails using your ship's helm—that is, your rational thinking. Record your responses in your journal. Consider all the people who could be involved in your achieving or not achieving your goal. Think again about who they are. What are their motives and how could you best enlist their help in achieving your goal? Make notes in your journal.

Plotting Your Course and Monitoring Your Progress

In planning your itinerary, estimate how long each step of your identified ports of call will take. Identify the prerequisite steps. A prerequisite step must be fully completed before you can embark on the next step. Truly question whether each step is a prerequisite to the next. Often we think linearly—that is, that things can only happen in a rigidly ordered sequence. This is not necessarily the case. The alternative is a chaotic sequence, in which there is no planning and activities occur in a random, higgledy-piggledy fashion. A combination of the two approaches is preferable: flexible thinking applied in an organised manner. We will call it *creative planning*.

Your planning should include a routine time and method for evaluating your progress. Set up a procedure whereby you regularly review your progress against the original planning horizon and monitor areas in which you are falling behind. These will let you know in advance which deadlines you are unlikely to achieve, and you can either plan to speed up the process or revisit your final completion dates. If this means inconveniencing anyone, you will be taking the initiative. You will be applying the Machiavellian principle of addressing a potential conflict at a time of your choice rather than having it forced upon you when you are less prepared. Being prepared to change and update your plan while en route indicates flexibility, initiative, and vision—all mature characteristics!

Know in advance that nothing goes perfectly to plan. However, a plan does provide you with advance insight when things begin to go awry, leaving you more time to manoeuvre into a better position and take appropriate action.

4.7 Activity: Plot and Monitor Progress of Your Goal

Return to your journal where you completed Activity 4.5. Complete this activity by following the steps below.

Step 1: Plan how and when you will achieve your goal. On your calendar, note your goal's crucial cut-off dates. Also identify which tasks may be linked to each other.

Step 2: Test your plan. Discuss it with a friend or someone you trust who will give you honest, reliable, and constructive feedback. Revisit your plan a day or two later. It is amazing how things settle after a good night's sleep, and a break also gives ideas lurking in your subconscious an opportunity to rise to the surface and present themselves. Ideas often go undeveloped and get lost if your thinking is cluttered and disorganised.

Step 3: Go public and make a contract. When you have your goal on your calendar and your planned contingencies in place, make a contract with another person committing to achieving your goal. The more you go public with your goals, the more likely you are to achieve them. Nothing acts as a greater incentive than making a public commitment. It also allows people you didn't initially identify as potential resources to come forward. I have had that experience repeatedly while developing this material.

The Value in Planning

Planning skills can be applied to many different situations, from writing a business letter to building a house. For example, in planning the sequence of how to present the information in this book, I followed a similar approach and formulated the outline course map. Although there were continuous amendments, the skeleton outline helped enormously and saved many hours of agonising over which content to cover in each leg of the journey and the appropriate sequence.

Initially, planning skills take time to master, and there is always the temptation to avoid the process and take a shortcut. However, with time and practice, it will become easier and quicker to apply. The long-term savings in time, money, and the reduction of the number of unpleasant surprises in your life will be more than sufficient reward to compensate for your discipline in applying the process.

When you do experience setbacks, try to keep in mind the big picture. Take a short break and return refreshed and determined to achieve your goal. If it was based on something that is truly meaningful to you originally, and within your belief and value system, the determination to attain it will soon be revived.

Craig Ballantyne

ETA: Your Estimated Time of Arrival

Consideration should be given to the estimated time period for each task and activity, and these can then be plotted on a calendar. To schedule things comfortably, build in some safety stops en route. Be realistic. Remember, the intention is to reduce stress and help you work more efficiently and effectively, not to add stress. Build in time for things to go wrong.

Start with your ideal completion date and work backward. By plotting the different activities on a calendar, you can see what needs to be done, when it needs to be done, and to what extent you are committed at any one time. It also lets you see, long in advance, if the exercise is indeed viable.

If you are being unrealistic in your expectations, you can adjust your time frame accordingly. This saves you from the stresses and strains of trying to cram everything in at the last minute and from last-minute disappointment.

When I was writing the course on which this book is based, my deadline was June. As I prepared my plan, it became obvious that if I wanted to have the course written and to test the material by June, I was not going to achieve my goal. I then made the alternative plan of test-driving (or sailing) the material already completed while still in the process of writing the final chapters. I started presenting the eight-week course in February and finished writing all of the material in March. This workable solution would not have arisen had I not planned in advance and thereby identified that my goal was not achievable without some creative and flexible thinking.

4.8 Activity: Develop an Action Plan

> Develop an action plan for one personal habit that you would like to adapt to a healthier, more efficient approach. Plan how you are going to address this and monitor your progress. Write up your plan in your journal.

In the next leg of your journey, you are going to look at maximising your two most important resources: time and money.

CHAPTER 5
Managing Your Treasures – Time and Money

Time is money.
> —Benjamin Franklin

Time is money says the proverb, but turn it around
and you get a precious truth. Money is time.
> —George Gissing

Being rich is having money; being
wealthy is having time.
> —Margaret Bonnano

Itinerary

In this chapter, you will learn about the coordinates of managing your time and financial resources, both essential in achieving your life goals.

Viewpoints

We will focus on:
- deductive and inductive reasoning
- focus of attention
- time management
- financial management

Introduction

In the previous chapter, we talked about identifying your life goals and, at the same time, we talked about managing your time and planning to achieve those goals by making space in your schedule. In this leg of the journey, we are going to develop this concept further by taking your financial resources into consideration, because both time and money play an integral role in reaching your destination. You will have the opportunity to evaluate your current use of these two resources—time and money—and how you can maximise this use in achieving your selected ports of call and the destination that you selected in the previous leg of your journey.

Time is essential for envisioning your goal, putting steps in place to achieve it, and then celebrating the achievement. Equally, financial resources are key to providing opportunity, flexibility, and the security to step out and do something new and different. Time and money often play an important role in the quality of your personal relationships and if not properly managed can become flashpoints and add to your stress in general.

How you spend your time and money are good indicators of your core values and beliefs. In the next activity, you will consider these attributes while monitoring your time. This snapshot of your life will form the foundation for further exercises, so try to be diligent in noting what activities you are involved in over the period of a week.

5.1 Activity: Consider How You Spend Your Time and Money

In your journal, record how you spend your time over the next seven days. Then, at the end of the week, answer the following questions:

- What beliefs and values does your time and money chart reflect?
- Are there any surprises for you?
- Is this reflective of your lifestyle viewed over a whole year?
- What areas should you consider reviewing?
- What motivates you to do these activities?

- Are you giving or receiving during these times, and is there a balance?
- What is your attitude during this time—is it positive or negative?
- Is it truly satisfying spending your time and money in this way?
- Are they intrinsic or extrinsic motivators?

Focusing and Finding Time

Many dreams remain unrealised simply because of perceived time constraints. Before expecting yourself to achieve more than you already do each day, let's look at Activity 3.3 you completed previously. How are you spending your time? What do your daily time sheets reflect? Consider what you are currently doing. Are your current activities aligned to where you want to be in the future? How can you best utilise your time in the future? Time is one of your most valuable resources.

5.2 Activity: Address Your Top Three Time-Wasters

Below is a list of typical time-wasters. Circle the time-wasters that relate to you. Although this list has been framed for a typical office environment, many of the items apply equally to the home situation. Once you have done this, in your journal, list your top three time-wasters. Consider how you could address them and thereby find more time in your day to allocate to achieving your life dreams and goals.

- insufficient planning and lack of objectives and priorities
- crisis management and shifting priorities
- attempting too much at once, unrealistic time estimates, and duplication of effort
- unclear or multiple reporting lines and incomplete or delayed information
- excessive paperwork, reading, and red tape
- poor systems with no standards, controls, or progress reports
- ineffective delegation, a need to over-control, wanting all facts, and making snap decisions
- inadequate equipment and resources
- meetings without clearly defined purposes and people not being kept informed
- poor communication and people not available for discussion
- lack of communication or over-communication
- failure to listen and lack of instructions
- visual distractions and noise
- untrained/inadequate team members and understaffed or overstaffed offices

- telephone interruptions
- drop-in visitors
- inability to say no
- personal disorganisation—cluttered desk/cupboard
- socialising and idle conversation
- lack of self-discipline, procrastination, and leaving tasks unfinished

Efficient and Effective Time-Management Tips

Efficient and effective time utilisation is a reflection of how in control you are of your life. It is useful to keep in mind the following two points:

1. Being *efficient* is doing the job *right*.
2. Being *effective* is doing the *right* job.

Outlined below is a list of tips that allow you to be more efficient and effective in utilising your time wisely. These tips will help you achieve your goals:

- Plan and set specific goals, including short, medium, and long-term.
- Write a to-do list, numbering the to-dos in order of priority and giving each a deadline.
- Know when to say no.
- Be persistent and finish the task the first time.
- Build in contingencies on deadlines.
- Handle paperwork once only.
- Screen calls.
- Shut your door when needed.
- Group phone calls near lunch or the end of day.
- Allocate yourself an uninterrupted quiet hour.

The concept of the quiet hour is simple. It calls for identifying a time segment, ranging from half an hour to two hours daily, during which you are on your own to reconnect with who you are and to plan where you are going. It is a space to relax and plan your time and activities. The quiet hour is simply uninterrupted quality time for *you*.

To achieve your goal, you will have to put time aside in your day, week, and month for it to become a reality. In the next activity, you are going to see if you can find possible improvements to the way you manage your day, allowing for the extra time to achieve your newly identified goal.

Financial Resources

Now let us look at your second treasure, money. In determining where you are placed on this asset, you will need to analyse your total income less your expenditures. Hopefully there will be a surplus, and if not, you will need a long-term plan to address this shortfall.

5.3 Activity: Establish Your Current Financial Position

In order to establish your financial position you will need to take a snapshot of where you are in terms of all of your income and compare that to all of your expenses over the same period of time.

Total income —	Total expenses =	Excess or shortfall

Step 1: Gather together as many documents and evidence for any income and expenses you incurred for the past year. Once you complete the activity, reflect in your journal on what you have found out about your current financial position.

Step 2: Determine your total income from all different sources. Work out your regular income over a specific period, the longer the better.

Type of income

- salary or wage (after tax)
- child support and other payments
- pension or government allowance
- regular interest from savings
- regular income from investments, such as an investment property, distributions from a managed fund, or dividends from shares

Total income _____

Savings attained

- emergence fund
- superannuation contributions
- general savings
- regular investments

Total savings _____

Step 3: Determine your expenses for the same period.

Household expenses

- rent
- repairs
- gas
- electricity
- water
- telephone/mobile
- rates
- body corporate fees
- Internet
- cable TV
- appliances
- groceries
- gardening

Subtotal _____

Education expenses

- school fees
- university/ college fees
- tuition
- books and uniforms
- camps and excursions

Subtotal _____

Debt repayments

- mortgage
- car loan
- other repayments
- credit cards
- personal loans
- store cards
- lay-bys

Subtotal _____

Transport expenses

- car registration
- parking
- fuel
- repairs/maintenance
- public transport

Subtotal _____

Personal expenses

- clothes and shoes
- hair and beauty
- massage
- gym

Subtotal _____

Medical expenses

- doctor
- dentist
- medicines

Subtotal _____

Insurances

- home and contents
- car
- health
- income protection
- life insurance

Subtotal _____

Contributions to savings

- emergency fund
- superannuation contributions
- general savings

- regular investments
- holiday projects

Subtotal _____

Other expenses

- childcare
- child-support payments
- gifts
- donations
- hobbies and sports
- subscriptions
- newspapers and magazines
- movies and DVDs
- restaurants and takeaways
- alcohol and cigarettes
- pet food
- other pet costs

Subtotal _____

Liabilities

- car
- mortgage
- other

Subtotal _____

Total your expenses and planned savings.

Step 4: Calculate your financial situation:

- Total income plus savings _____
- Less total expenses and liabilities _____
- Surplus/deficit _____

Adapted from *Understanding Money: How to Make It Work for You issued by the Australian Government*

Strategies for Financial Security and Suggestions to Ensure Successful Life Change

Although money cannot buy happiness, it does provide some security, flexibility and freedom for us to choose between a number of different destinations. The following are some suggestions on how to explore ways of managing this treasure.

Save and Invest

There are many different ways of investing, and there is wisdom in having a number of different plans so as to accommodate different short-term and long-term goals.

Research is an integral part of making wise savings and investment decisions. It is an opportunity to fully apply the helm—your questioning techniques of what, where, how, who, which, and so on.

Plan for Retirement

I went to a talk on retirement recently during which the guest speaker strongly advocated that we should be investing in enjoying our careers and planning to work for as long as we are fit and able. Research shows that people who are fit and active tend to be healthier and to live longer. He went on to explain that with the amazing advances in science, people are living longer and longer, and this trend is likely to continue, and so we need to plan on working and supporting ourselves for a longer period of time.

Researching what rules apply to you ensures that you make the right choice in deciding which fund to invest in and how to maximise the long-term benefits. Decisions on which superfund to choose should be made with a long-term perspective. The risks and benefits, as well as the annual fees and costs, need to be taken into consideration when making the decision. It's a perfect opportunity to apply a decision matrix. (see Activity 4.4)

5.4 Activity: Research your life expectancy

Go to www.helpage.org/global-agewatch/popultion-ageing-data, enter your country, and review how long you are expected to live. Also consider what portion of the population will make up that age category. In your journal, consider who will be funding your retirement and note your retirement plan. If you don't have a plan, consider what might it consist of.

5.5 Activity: Identify Ways to Improve Management of Your Finances

Circle which of the following tips you are currently applying in the management your finances. Use a highlighter to select other tips that you could implement now to assist you in managing your finances.

- Make sure income exceeds expenditure.
- Develop a realistic budget.
- Build in a cushion of money for when things go wrong.
- Have definite goals that you are saving for, as this helps in putting off impulse purchases.
- Keep a spending diary.
- Check for leaks in what you are spending your money on.
- Keep all your bills and statements in one place.
- Review your whole financial situation at least once a year.
- Identify what is essential in your expenses and what are extras that could possibly be curtailed.
- Have only one credit card with the lowest possible interest rate
- Keep your credit limit within what you can easily afford to repay
- Pay off your credit card prior to being charged interest
- Consolidate your debt. If you are struggling to meet your repayments, approach the institution concerned, explain your position, and work out a way to manage the situation. It is better to approach them than to wait for them to approach you.
- Try to own more than you owe.
- Plan your menu for the week.
- Make a shopping list.
- Don't shop when hungry.
- Make it difficult to access savings.
- Arrange for automatic deductions into your savings account.
- Research the best and most cost-effective savings options. For example, how much you earn and how much tax you pay will affect which is the best savings option for you.
- Consider fees and other charges as well as the potential risks when choosing your savings option.
- Have different savings accounts for different goals or projects.
- Make your money work for you, for example by purchasing an investment property.
- Don't put all your eggs in one basket—have diverse methods of saving.
- Take your lunch to work.
- Repair shoes/appliances/clothes.

- Share clothes.
- Shop online.
- Consider prepaid options.
- Rent, hire or borrow instead of buying items that you only use occasionally.
- Look at your expenses and see where you can get a better deal. Recently I reduced my internet/telephone fees by 90 per cent simply by phoning my service provider, suggesting that the current fee structure was excessive, and asking if they could improve their service-fee costs.
- Bring down loans as quickly as possible.
- Get advice from the experts.
- Arrange for all of your debts to be in one place.
- Reduce debt that is not positive debt (good debt is debt that has a potential long-term value—for example, a mortgage on a house.
- Leave your credit card at home or secure it in the deepfreeze to limit impulse buying
- Be careful with whom you shop. I know shopping with my daughter leads to many impulse purchases—and not always for me!
- When out, only take money you can afford to spend at that time, leave the rest at home.

Consider Good Debt—Asset-Based Debt

Some debt that helps you to secure valuable assets—for example, a house—can be useful. In this situation, consider carefully what you can afford, with a built-in cushion as a hedge against increasing interest rates due to changing economic conditions. Choosing a loan with the lowest interest rate with a reputable organisation is wise. Explore potential hidden costs.

5.6 Activity: Better Managing Your Finances

In your journal, make a note of which three factors you would like to introduce or focus on and what your short-term and long-term financial goals may be. Explore how you intend to achieve them and how will you monitor your progress.

Consult the Experts

When entering a difficult port, it is wise to enlist the help of a pilot boat to bring you into harbour; when crossing a hazardous sea, it is prudent to seek the guidance of a skilled navigator who has intimate knowledge of the waters, currents and hazards that may be invisible under the water. Skilled navigators have a deep knowledge of long-term economic and weather patterns and conditions that will be useful in making these plans.

Likewise, it is wise to speak to a number of different qualified sources to make sure you gain a whole perspective and a balanced view of what options are available to you when navigating the financial waters. Expert advice need not be costly, with many institutions or organisations offering it as part of their service. Qualified advice can significantly maximise your knowledge and position. Prior to attending your meeting, ensure that the person giving you advice is licensed and qualified to do so; explore how he or she derives an income and what the costs may be to you.

Be wary of schemes that offer get-rich-quick options. History has shown these to be mostly scams, whereby you provide the opportunity for someone else to get rich quickly!

5.7 Activity: Explore the MoneySmart Web Site

Go to http://www.moneysmart.gov.au and explore the information available to help you to track and make decisions on your finances. In your journal, reflect on the changes you intend to make in your spending and saving behaviour and when you are planning to review these changes.

Change Personal Habits

Changing personal habits is an extremely difficult process. It takes at least six weeks of concentrated effort practicing the desired new behaviour before it starts to become a habit. The following are five steps to breaking bad habits, or alternatively five steps to developing good habits:

1. Recognise the difficulty in changing personal habits.
2. Develop a better way of doing things.
3. Launch the new habit strongly: go public and tell someone. This will give you a sense of commitment, and you will gain support.
4. Practice the new habit often.
5. Allow no exceptions.

Achieving your life goals and dreams also requires resilience and energy, and ways to minimise your stress and maximising your vital energy. In the next leg of your journey, we are going to examine how you manage your stress and preserve your sailing craft.

CHAPTER 6

Enhancing Your Vital Energy

Eternal Autumn Leaves

Merrily, merrily dance through the trees,
And waltz with the wind, graceful autumn leaves!
Playing your games as you float to the ground:
Chasing your playmates in circles around:
For once you were buds on tender green shoots,
Nourished by sap that swelled up from the roots.
Do you remember those mornings in May?
When clapping your hands to the new-born day,
You sang to the flowers, spoke to the birds,
And felt a great joy unexpressed by words.
You know as you fall, your end is not here—
You are immortal, with nothing to fear:
The soil that's nourished you will, one day,
Bring forth your offspring to start on their way.
What is more glorious than the mind can conceive,
Is the spirit dwelling in mortal weave:
The Infinite, enfolding buds in May,
Still holds to His bosom your living clay.
Since all that is you can never be lost,
Go singing to God as you're tossed and tossed:
Thank Him, above all, that nothing is lost.

—Safeya Moyein

Itinerary

In this chapter, you will assess your current level of fitness and mental health, understand the relationship of positive and negative stressors in your life, and learn how best to cope with these factors.

Viewpoints

You will focus on:
- health
- environmental awareness
- social awareness
- stress management

Travel bag

You will need:
- your journal
- orange, yellow, and red highlighters
- a quiet private place to practice relaxing
- access to the Internet

Introduction

To function at your full potential means performing to the maximum of your abilities at all times. In order to achieve this, you need to be fit, dynamic, energetic, and full of vital energy. *Vital energy* can be described as your life-force energy and it is fundamental and crucial to your survival. It determines the speed (measured in knots) at which you are able to sail. People with an abundance of life-force energy are enthusiastic and energetic. They are inspired and their exuberance for life is often contagious and invigorating to those around them.

Nutrition is also an important factor in determining your level of health, and this will be explored in the next leg of our journey. For this chapter, I have chased seven different dimensions that combine to determine how effectively you are utilising and exercising your vital energy and reaching your full potential. These personal dimensions are:

- cognitive ability
- physical health
- emotional well-being
- mental ability
- social integration
- spirituality
- environment

In reality, these dimensions are not finite and can be represented on a continuum:

The Vital Energy Health Continuum

Dimensions

	Minimum potential		Maximum potential
Cognitive ability	Unfocused	_____	Focused
Physical health	Disease	_____	Ease
Emotional well-being	Unstable	_____	Stable
Social integration	Alienated	_____	Integrated
Spirituality awareness	Closed	_____	Enlightened
Environment	Unsupportive	_____	Supportive (safe)

Your *carrying capacity* is your natural physical, emotional and cognitive strength. It is determined by your genetic makeup and the social and environmental context into which you are born. This, combined with your life experience and your ability to cope with and regenerate your vital energy reserves, determines your position as you progress through life. We will discuss this in more detail later in this chapter.

Craig Balantyne

Generating and Maintaining Vital Energy

All systems—be they living organisms, human organisations, or larger social structures—need to maintain a homeostatic condition. In other words, they need to be maintained in some form of balance or equilibrium. Once this homeostatic balance is disrupted, feedback and control mechanisms come into play to restore it. Systems are dynamic, circular, interactive, and creating transactional effects. At no time is a system in a static state. Our systems include:

- electrolytes
- cells
- the circulatory and lymphatic systems
- the respiratory system
- the digestive system
- the urinary system
- the nervous system
- the endocrine system
- the reproductive system
- the skeletal, joint, and muscular systems
- the community in which we live

The community in which you live is itself a system and an integral part of who you are. The scope of your community depends on your perception. It could extend from your nuclear family to your extended family, neighbourhood, nation, continent, globe, even the universe! I believe that our vital energy is interrelated with all of these.

We are electrochemical beings. If we had too much or too little potassium, our hearts would stop. All systems, by definition, involve energy transformation—that is, the intake of one form of energy and a processing and then output of another form of energy.

You can have a high level or a low level of vital energy, or something in between. Ideally, all systems should be in balance and operating at a high level. Your position on the vital-energy continuum is determined by your carrying capacity and the stressors to which you are exposed, including life circumstances and life events; the context, cumulative, and ripple effects of these; and finally, how you cope with them—positively or negatively.

Eustress and Distress

"Stress" is anything that stimulates the body and these stimulants can be either negative stressors (distress) and / or positive stressors (eustress), and occur in every dimension of your life. The term *eustress* was first used by endocrinologist Hans Selye in 1978, when he published a model dividing stress into two major categories: eustress (usually related to desirable events) and distress. (negative events or stimuli).

These stressors are omnipresent and life is a dynamic cybernetic system. It is a product of being alive: all living organisms experience stress. A stressor disrupts the physical, mental, emotional, social and spiritual homeostasis of the individual. The resulting response may be physical, mental, emotional, or any combination of these, for example, an increased heart rate, a sense of anxiety, or social withdrawal.

Stressors can occur from the most microscopic scale of biochemical reaction, such as chemical air and water pollutants, to the macro scale of catastrophic events like an earthquake. Stress is a factor of life—it is how we deal with it that is important in determining the level of negative impact it has on our health and the quality of our lives. In the sailing-craft analogy, this could be barnacles growing on the hull of the boat, or rusting and fraying occurring as a result of weathering, or the impact of a huge wind or wave knocking us completely off course.

As we have evolved, the stressors in our environment have changed. For example, in relatively recent evolutionary history, *homo sapiens* had to contend with direct threats to survival, such as being eaten alive or killed by marauding tribes. Consequently, our instinctive and automatic responses were for fight, flight or freeze. In fact, there are over two thousand chemical pathways in the body, each with different and often interrelated functions and the mechanics of these pathways are still not fully understood. They help gear up the body for dramatic physical action—for example, the release of adrenaline and noradrenaline causes an increase in the heart and breathing rate. However, this preparation for regular but unpredictable surges of physical energy is often no longer appropriate, and in modern times, there is often limited scope for this generated energy to be dissipated, leaving us with a feeling of anxiety and tension. This balance can be seen in the illustration.

Modern man has not evolved physiologically to respond appropriately to our altered living environment with its typical current-day stressors. Appropriate coping responses have to be learned to manage situations positively and to find suitable ways of releasing the tension generated in muscles conditioned by evolution to prepare for physical action.

The Balance between Eustress and Distress

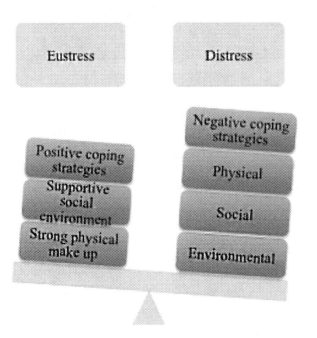

Ease-Disease Continuum

A stressor causes a state of tension and, if incorrectly managed, can be potentially pathogenic. Alternatively, if properly managed, it can have neutral or even healthy (eustress) consequences. It is the effective or ineffective management of this tension through coping behaviours that determines and affects your position on the ease-disease continuum. Think about the stressors in your life, and let's look at how you can positively cope with these on a day-to-day basis.

Stressors that threaten the balance of the individual can be positive. For example, getting married or having a big family gathering can be challenging and happy while still being stressful. Your needs and perceptions largely determine the weight or impact of a stressor.

Responses to stressors can be stressors in their own right. For example, after a long day at the office you may come home and have a drink and a cigarette. Both of these behavioural coping responses will help to relax you and let you unwind. They are, however, stressors in their own right. The cigarette will impact on you negatively by damaging your teeth and blood vessels with nicotine, increasing your heart rate, and lining your lungs with tar. The obvious negative effects of these stressors may only be experienced years later in the form of coronary artery disease or cancer.

It is important to note that these dimensions are potentially distinctive. For example, a person dying from cancer who has the right frame of mind as well as physical and social support can be in excellent emotional and spiritual health. Equally, a physically healthy person who is lacking social support and has poor coping skills could be depressed and on the *disease* side of the mental ease-disease continuum. By being aware of the positive and negative elements of stress, you can start to develop a positive and healthy way of life. You can begin to actively manage and combat stress by reducing its negative impact, thereby maintaining a proactive and preventative health-care lifestyle. This is illustrated in "The Vital-Energy Exchange Equation" diagram.

The Vital Energy Exchange Equation

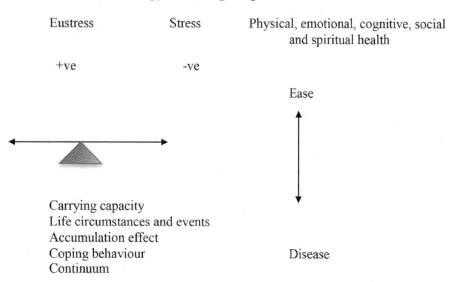

Eustress   Stress   Physical, emotional, cognitive, social and spiritual health

+ve   -ve

Ease

Carrying capacity
Life circumstances and events
Accumulation effect
Coping behaviour
Continuum

Disease

The combination of factors is illustrated in the "Summary Stress Model" diagram.

Summary Stress Model

Influencing Factors of Carrying capacity, Stress, Coping strategies, and the Out Come on the Ease – Disease Continuum

Coping strategies + ve and - ve

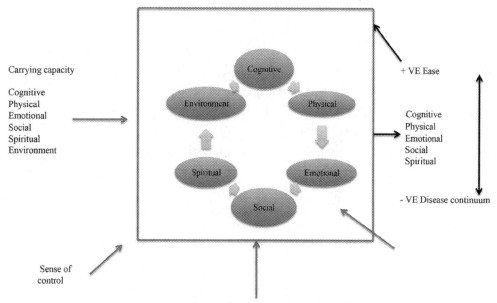

Carrying capacity

Cognitive
Physical
Emotional
Social
Spiritual
Environment

Cognitive

Environment   Physical

Spiritual   Emotional

Social

+ VE Ease

Cognitive
Physical
Emotional
Social
Spiritual

~ VE Disease continuum

Sense of control

Stressors from microscopic to macroscopic

Strength and Design: Your Carrying Capacity

We are all born with a physical genetic carrying capacity and we are only as strong as our weakest biological and physiological link. This includes characteristics like physical makeup and level of intelligence, though neither of these factors is permanently fixed. The physical well-being of our bodies is constantly monitored by a highly sophisticated immunological surveillance network that, if fully operational, protects us from disease.

Our carrying potential is the combination of the capabilities with which we have been born and the cumulative effect of our life experience to date. Factors we are born with include our genetic strengths and vulnerabilities, our level of intelligence and physical aptitude, and our social and environmental context.

6.1 Activity: Look at Your Chosen Mode of Transport

In Chapter 3, you created your own sailing-craft model. You may have done a sketch of it or actually made your own. Revisit it and then answer the following questions:

- What is it? Is it old or new, well used or with low mileage?
- What type of utilities does it have? What type of work is it designed to do? Is it modern and sleek, or stout and long-lasting?
- What colours did you choose? Are they purely functional, being specifically task-orientated, or gay and full of energy?
- How much extra cargo are you carrying?
- What fuel do you use?
- What motivates you?
- Does your craft require some maintenance?

This potential or capability of a type of craft is similar to our carrying potential and the degree to which we develop it as we travel through life. Some of us are good at mathematics; others have great beauty or physical strength; still others a great capacity to care and nurture. In essence, our carrying potential determines our strengths and our weaknesses and it is our weaknesses, plus life stressors, that predispose us to certain diseases more than others.

Environment, Setting, and the Elements: Your Life Circumstances

Your life circumstances include the environment into which you were born, your stage of life, the events to which you have been exposed and the resources to which you have access—including wealth and other material resources, education, available medical services, geographic location, place of residence and available space. It also includes the level of your social support network—for example, marriage (particularly important for a man), close family and friends, pets, church membership, work environment, and informal and formal group associations.

Environmental factors include the physical environment, such as temperature, atmosphere, air pollution and free radicals. It encompasses the air you breathe and the food you eat. Biological organisms, bacteria, and viruses are all part of the environment and may be either helpful or destructive.

Life events include marriage; death of a spouse; divorce; change of job, home or country; or, in the extreme, an earthquake! I am sure you could add a few of your own. All of these elements have the potential of being either draining (a stressor) or supportive, recharging your resources and energizing you (a eustressor). Eustressors leave you feeling uplifted and energised, adding to your inner resources rather than depleting them.

Social Context: Your Travelling Companions

Travelling companions are those people we share our journey with—our family, circle of friends, or work colleagues and associates. By understanding the impact stressors have on our whole life, we will be able to better manage our life and its vital energy. As mentioned earlier, the community in which we live is an integral part of who we are. In your case, this includes your partner, your nuclear family, and your extended family. It also includes your neighbours and the people you work with. On a larger scale, it includes your country and, finally, the world. What happens in each of these spheres affects you to a greater or lesser extent. You also make a reciprocal impact, even if only in a small way.

To illustrate the dynamic elements of this system, think of a wheel. Each spoke of the wheel represents one of these factors, as shown in the illustration.

Integration Wheel

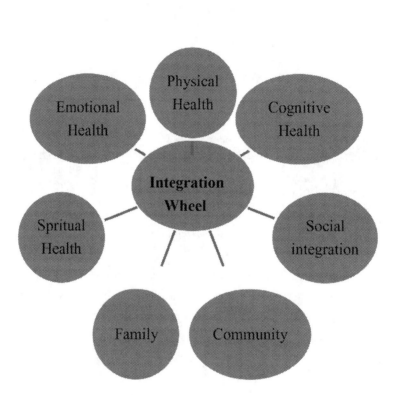

The more integrated you are along these differing dimensions, the larger the spokes and the greater your potential for movement, and the further you will go with the minimum of effort. Alternately, if some spokes are short or non-existent, the wheel will still be able to turn but not as fluidly, and it runs the risk of becoming entrenched and static. In the next exercise, think about the extent to which you are integrated into each of these dimensions.

6.2 Activity: Draw Your Personal Integration Wheel

Draw the integrated wheel in your journal and, on each of the spokes, mark your position on a potential rating of 0 to 10. Then draw in the rim of your wheel.

Integration Wheel

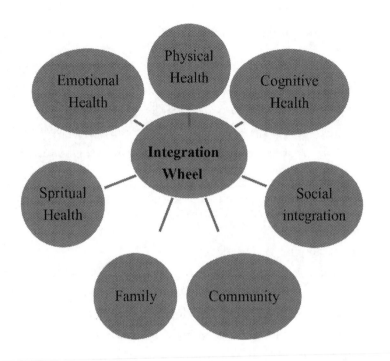

In your journal, answer the following questions:

- Where are you fully extended, and where is there room for improvement?
- How smoothly does your wheel rotate?
- How well do you think each system of your life functions, and what improvements could you make?

Sense of Control

Research has shown that individuals who feel in control of their lives do not report feeling or experiencing stress. This sense of control has a pervading influence on our view of the world and our role in it.

Accumulative Effect of Stressors

The accumulative nature of stressors takes into account when the stressors occur and the magnitude of the event. Stressors that occur at the same time have an exponential impact on the person, as the combined effects are greater than the individual consequences of each stressor (that is, the whole is greater than the sum of its parts). For example, a man experiencing the loss of his wife, his home, and his income simultaneously would be under far greater stress than if those events had occurred at ten-year intervals.

6.3 Activity: Assess Your Current Level of Stress

Looking at the "Inventory of Distressors and Eustressors," circle which ones apply to you. Use highlighters to note whether they are positive (yellow), negative (red), or both (orange). Once you have given some thought to the extent of negative and positive stress in your life, use your journal to reflect on the physical mental, and emotional strain of excessive stress—which happens when the equation tips in favour of the negative elements.

Inventory of Distressors and Eustressors

1. Individual Carrying Potential
   - Congenital (existing from birth): good/poor nutrition while *in utero*, biological and psychological factors affecting the mother during pregnancy, physical strength/deformity, intelligence/limited intellectual ability, strong genes/faulty genetic structure of DNA, prone to good health (e.g. good teeth)/prone to disease (e.g. cancer, heart disease)
   - Developmental: early development—enriched/deprived physical, psychological and social environment
   - Stage in life cycle: examinations, marriage, buying a house, birth of a child, midlife crisis, retirement, empty-nest syndrome, awareness of physical ageing
   - Demographic status: class, race, religion, minority/majority group

2. Behavioural/psychological
   - Personality: Type A personality, workaholic, inappropriate/appropriate goals, needs and desires, external/internal locus of control, aggressive/passive/assertive, extreme needs for power/content, ambition, perfectionism, fear of failure/success
   - Cognitive: good/poor problem-solving ability, inappropriate/appropriate coping responses, positive/negative life perception, perceived lack of return on emotional and psychological investments, role conflict, no moral or religious beliefs, good/poor self-concept, resolved/unresolved personal conflicts, guilt, independent/dependent, anger, fear, perfectionism, obsessive or incongruent thoughts and feelings

- Lifestyle: poor/good diet, lack of/regular exercise, healthy living, poor/good sleeping habits, alcohol abuse, smoking, drug abuse, disruption of natural rhythms, inappropriate/appropriate coping behaviours

3. Spiritual
    - Existential reality: religious and moral beliefs, awareness of one's own mortality, death of a family member or close friend

4. Environmental
    - Physical: lighting, noise, housing, geographical location and space, humidity, cold, heat, vibration, extreme temperatures, continuous movement, harmful chemicals, soothing, clean, safe, healthy
    - Macro physical: famine, drought, war, economic recession, natural disasters, secure, safe, predictable
    - Biochemical: polluting poisons, safe, clean
    - Biotic: bacteria, viruses
    - Occupational: employed/unemployed, environment fit, career reaching a plateau, good career fit, limited decision-making and latitude, work rate too fast or too slow, dangerous work, ergonomically designed tools, equipment, workplace, career.
    - Social: traditional structures in the community network (the extended family), changing work practices, and greater social and geographical mobility

5. Context
    - Timing of the stressors: in rapid succession; ripple and/or cumulative effect; inter-exposure (insufficient recovery time); changes of house, job, town or country; well-spaced; manageable

6. Social
    - Social: social change, crime, political instability, vandalism, crowding, interpersonal conflict, connection, family security, sense of belonging and safety
    - Personal: marital and family conflict, secure family, undesirable/desirable parent models, role ambiguity, pathogenic family structures, separation, divorce, isolation, maladaptive/adaptive behaviour of peer group, legal disputes/conflicts, death of a spouse or friend, unresolved past conflicts, irrational communication, family and class pressure, supportive family
    - Social network: poor personal relationships (with family, friends, and work colleagues), feelings of isolation, feeling connected

To date, an enormous amount of research has focused on the pathological side of health and how excessive stress damages health.

Inventory of Physiological and Psychological Consequences of Stress

There appears to be an endless list of diseases and symptoms that scientific research has linked to everyday life stressors. These cause us enormous physiological and psychological health issues. In the activity below, you will determine your level of stress-related ill health.

6.4 Activity: Determine Your Level of Stress-Related Ill Health

All of the symptoms and diseases listed below have been linked through published research to stress. In order to identify the number of stress-related symptoms and diseases that you have experienced, circle the ones you have experienced in the last three years. Then, in your journal, answer the questions at the end of the activity.

- headaches and migraines
- constant back pain; muscular pains; tension in jaw, neck, shoulders
- constant sweaty palms, allergies, asthma
- loss of appetite, nausea, eating disorders (bulimia nervosa, anorexia nervosa)
- diarrhoea and/or constipation
- change in weight, obesity
- premature greying of hair, loss of hair
- burnout
- insomnia
- anxiety or panic attacks
- depression and/or nervous breakdown
- disorganized, inability to concentrate, forgetfulness
- feelings of being smothered, hopelessness, guilt, sadness, pessimism
- feelings of loneliness, helplessness, restlessness, floating anxiety
- feelings of unreality, irritability, being accident-prone
- loss of empathy, emotional exhaustion, moodiness, apathy
- fatigue—feeling constantly tired, jelly legs, dizziness, trembling, shaking
- nervous tic, stuttering breathlessness, hyperventilation
- irregular menstrual cycle, hot and cold flashes
- sexual dysfunction
- problems with infertility
- complications with pregnancy

- heart disease, e.g. chest pains/discomfort, heart palpitations, irregular/fast/slow heartbeat, hypertension, coronary heart disease, intermittent high blood pressure, arteriosclerosis, heart attack, angina
- change in blood sugar levels or diabetes
- cancer or stroke
- alcoholism, other addictions, drug abuse
- obsessive compulsive behaviour
- phobias—agoraphobia, social phobia (afraid of being outside or other people)
- influenza, colds, bronchitis, peptic ulcer
- spastic colon
- lipid abnormalities
- rheumatoid arthritis
- psoriasis, dermatitis, eczema
- colitis
- enuresis
- thyrotoxicosis
- narcolepsy
- contemplating suicide

In your journal, consider the following:

- Are you surprised about how many stressors you have experienced? Why or why not?
- In your present travels on your journey of self-discovery, which of these stressors are currently impacting on your mental and physical health?
- What constructive coping behaviours and life changes could you consider making to positively enhance your health?

Rejuvenating and Nurturing Your Craft

Now that you have considered the stressors in your life and the consequences that you are already experiencing, think about how you cope with these stressors. Remember that the long-term effects of stress often present when people are in their late forties or fifties, at a time when the damage is extensive and the repair work difficult to implement. It makes much more sense to apply a preventative sooner, rather than a remedial approach later.

Consider, for example, the sailing craft. It is logical to varnish the hull of a boat regularly to protect it from the elements of wind, sun, water and barnacles, than to wait until it has sprung a leak. Trying to remove the dry rot, barnacles, and rust by sanding down and cutting out the rotten wood at a later date is also more costly and demands more effort. While the repair work is underway, the boat is not functional and has to be taken out of the water. Need I say more?

Stressors appear on many different levels, from the micro-organisms that eat away at the wood of the boat to the major catastrophic events that impact us on various levels from our micro-chemical pathways to our physical structure. Further, stressors can have a cumulative effect. The single barnacle has little effect on the hull of the boat, yet if left for twenty years and joined by a colony of other barnacles, it will have a dramatic impact. Simple coping behaviours, such as regularly painting the boat, build up a level of resistance and can stave off the impact of stressors in the long-term. This in-built reserve is called eustress, which we have discussed earlier in this chapter. Preventative measures are generally called *positive coping behaviours*.

Ironically, many of the coping behaviours we utilise may be effective in helping us deal with stress at that specific time, but by their very nature, they have the capacity to become stressors in their own right over a long period of time. Smoking or drinking alcohol makes us feel more relaxed, but the long-term effects of these are just as damaging to the body as the barnacle to the boat. They look quite harmless on the surface and in isolation, but with time and in excess they can be as devastating and as damaging as a tornado.

Coping with Stress

There are three ways of coping with stress:

1. prevention
2. tolerance
3. release of tension

Coping behaviours can be physical, emotional, mental, social, or spiritual, and include your:

- cognitive skills, i.e. analysing and assessing the situation
- perceptual responses
- sense of control over events
- value system
- behavioural response and the actions you take
- physiological responses, such as breathing and heart rates

Again, these coping responses can be negative or positive.

Research has shown that the mind generates the same physiological responses in a person, whether an event is real or imagined. It is therefore very important that you learn to control your thoughts and the way that you approach a stressor. For example, the same stressor will create a different chemical and therefore a different physiological response depending on whether a person sees the stressor positively, as a challenge, or negatively, as a threat. Furthermore, the severity of a disease and the speed of recovery are also largely determined by the sick person's outlook. Those with a positive outlook recover more quickly and completely.

Eustress helps you to rejuvenate your resources and your reserves. Examples of positive coping behaviours—that is, eustress generators—are listed below. I am sure you can add ideas of your own.

Positive Coping Behaviours

- healthy eating—this will be explored further on the next leg of your journey
- appropriate weight for physical attributes and age
- sufficient sleep and establishing a routine
- plenty of drinking water and regular exercise
- regular mental activity and meaningful occupation
- limited stimulant intake (e.g. of alcohol, drugs, coffee)
- goals and aspirations that match your capabilities
- congruent lifestyle—personal values, goals, and lifestyle complementary, matching work and home environment
- peaceful living environment and doing something creative
- listening to music, dancing, and taking on hobbies and interests that help you to unwind
- spiritual affiliation and growth, relaxation, meditation, and yoga
- marriage, intimate relationships, friends, and a sense of community
- good social support and network, and renewing old ties
- owning and caring for pets
- determining stress-tolerance level and living within those boundaries
- allowing yourself to be human, laughing, and having a good sense of humour
- unscheduled time in your diary (at least one day a month) to play and have fun
- positive thinking and using appropriate problem-solving techniques
- reappraisal of the situation and rationalising an emotive situation
- holidays and time spent in natural surroundings
- anticipating the response of the environment and avoiding potentially stressful situations
- writing a gratitude journal and reading inspirational books
- being involved in charity work and helping others

6.5 Activity: Positive Coping Mechanisms in Handling Stress

Although all individuals are subjected to stress in their daily lives, some appear to be better able to cope effectively with stress, and as a result they tend to be physically and mentally healthier. Consider your current forms of coping behaviour:

- Are they preventative, helping you tolerate the situation or helping you release tension as a result of the stressors?
- Are they positive or negative coping behaviours?

- Are their long-term effects for your health positive or negative?
- What other coping behaviours could you be using?

Coping with stress in a positive way allows you to create reserves. These reserves increase the chances of your being on the positive side of the ease-disease continuum. They improve your potential carrying capacity and leave you better equipped to tackle future stressors.

6.6 Activity: Test Your Coping Skills

How do you cope with stress? There are many ways, but some are more effective than others. This stress scale was created largely on the basis of results compiled by clinicians and researchers who tried to identify how people effectively cope with stress. It is an educational tool designed to inform you of the most effective and healthy ways to cope. In your journal, write down the points you receive for each criteria outlined below.

- Give yourself 10 points if you feel you have supportive family around you.
- Give yourself 10 points if you actively pursue a hobby.
- Give yourself 10 points if you belong to a social club or activity group in which you participate more than once a month.
- Give yourself 15 points if you are within 4.5 kilograms of your ideal body weight, considering your height and bone structure.
- Give yourself 15 points if you practice some form of deep relaxation at least five times a week. Deep relaxation includes meditation, progressive muscle relaxation, imagery, and yoga.
- Give yourself 5 points for each time you exercise for 30 minutes or longer during an average week.
- Give yourself 5 points for each nutritionally balanced and wholesome meal you eat during an average day. A nutritionally balanced meal is low in fat and high in vegetables, fruits, and whole-grain products.
- Give yourself 5 points if you do something you really enjoy and that is just for you during an average week.
- Give yourself 10 points if you have a place in your home where you can go to relax or be by yourself.
- Give yourself 10 points if you practice time-management techniques daily.
- Subtract 10 points for each pack of cigarettes you smoke during an average day.
- Subtract 5 points for each evening during an average week on which you use any form of medication or chemical substance, including alcohol, to help you sleep.

- Subtract 10 points for each day during an average week on which you consume any form of medication or chemical substance, including alcohol, to reduce anxiety or just to calm down.
- Subtract 5 points for each evening during an average week that you bring work home—work meant to be done at your place of employment.

Now calculate your total score. A perfect score is 115. If you scored in the 50–60 range, you probably have adequate coping skills for most common stress. However, keep in mind that the higher your score, the greater your ability to cope with stress in an effective, healthy manner.

This stress assessment was created by Dr. George Everly Jr. of the University of Maryland. It is reprinted from a US Public Health Service pamphlet *What Do You Know About Stress* (DHHS Publication No. PHS79-50097) and is in the public domain. The Holistic Development Exchange has a health and success website that you may like to look at to find techniques for cultivating physical and mental health and achieving success. Follow http://www.wholisticdev.com/Stress-Management-Tips.shtml to a page titled "Techniques for Health and Success" that you may find helpful.

Keeping Your Craft Stress-Free

One of the best ways of coping with stress is to put time aside every day to relax. In fact, relaxation is accessible to us all and is one of the easiest coping mechanisms to include in your lifestyle. The next activity will guide you through a number of different relaxation techniques that you can try and see which ones work for you.

There is nothing profound in these relaxation techniques. What will be profound is if you manage to apply relaxation in your lifestyle on a regular basis. We should have fifteen to twenty minutes of relaxation twice a day, ideally at sunrise and sundown. Once this becomes a regular habit, the positive benefits will be enormous, in every aspect of your life. The key is in the application.

There are a number of suggestions explained in the following activity on achieving a relaxed state through focusing on your breathing, clearing your mind of irrelevant thoughts, and consciously helping your muscles release tension. As you achieve a deeper level of relaxation, your breathing will slow down and become deeper, body temperature and blood pressure will be reduced, and your energy system will have the opportunity to recharge.

6.7 Activity: Learning Relaxation Techniques

There are many different ways of consciously relaxing. Try the techniques included in this section or a combination and then record your experiences in your journal. The technique of learning to relax takes time, and you will need to practice the techniques daily for at least two weeks before you can honestly assess their benefits.

Preparing to Relax and Getting Comfortable

Find a quiet and peaceful place with few distractions and no disruptions. The ideal spot should be private, and you should allow sufficient time. Relaxation is also best done before eating or at least two hours after a meal, as your digestive system creates a tension of its own which, while at work, is not conducive to the rest of your body relaxing. Your clothing should be loose; you should remove your belt, shoes, glasses, contact lenses, and jewellery—in fact, anything that makes you feel restricted and uncomfortable. You could then question why you had them on in the first place!

Now choose a position. It is important that it is a position in which you feel unthreatened and comfortable. Suggested postures are:

- sitting in an easy chair
- supine position—lying on the ground with your neck supported by a small cushion or rolled towel, with or without your arms slightly raised by pillows
- supine position—with your legs raised by cushions under the knees or supported by the seat of a chair
- seated upright in a chair

Your body should be spread so that each of your limbs is positioned separately. This means no crossing of arms or legs. Your body should be in a balanced alignment, with your head carefully balanced at the top of your spine. It is important that the body is supported as much as possible, particularly when first practicing relaxation techniques. In time, as you become more proficient, you should be able to relax your muscles in almost any position and achieve this even when you are in an unpleasant situation, for example, in a situation of confrontation.

The objective of relaxation is to reduce the activity in the cerebral cortex and the central nervous system and to give the muscles an opportunity to relax and rest. This can be achieved in one of two ways:

- focus on relaxing the muscles and the mind will become less active
- calm the mind and the muscles will relax

Either approach works, and both are discussed below. Breathing is also discussed and is an important aspect of both approaches. We will first approach relaxation through focusing on your various muscles.

Relaxing Your Muscles

1. Ensure that you are in a comfortable position and that your body is in alignment and your head is balanced. Close your eyes.

2. Tune into your breathing. Breathe in slowly and calmly, pause, breathe out slowly and calmly, pause. As you exhale, say to yourself *r-e-l-a-x*. Feel yourself sinking into the supporting environment—the chair, the carpet, or the bed.

3. Now turn your attention to your feet. As you inhale, flex your feet up toward you as tightly as you can. Hold the position for a few seconds.

4. On exhalation, relax your feet to their natural resting position. Feel the relaxation in your leg and thigh muscles.

5. On inhalation, point the feet away from you, as rigidly and as tightly as you can. Hold the position and feel the tension.

6. On exhalation, relax your feet to their natural resting position. Feel the relaxation.

7. Now turn your attention to your legs. As you inhale, tighten the muscles in your legs and buttocks as tightly as you can. Hold the position for a few seconds.

8. On exhalation, relax your feet to their natural resting position. Feel the relaxation in your leg and thigh muscles.

9. Concentrate on your hands. On inhalation, grip your hands into a fist, as tightly as you can. Hold the position and feel the tension.

10. On exhalation, relax your hands to their natural resting position. Feel the relaxation.

11. On inhalation, expand your hands, spreading your fingers apart. Hold the position.

12. On exhalation, relax your hands to their natural resting position. Feel the relaxation.

13. Focus your attention on your neck and shoulder muscles. With your next inhalation, roll your head down and curve your shoulders inward as tightly as you can. Hold the position for a few moments.

14. Exhale and relax to your natural position. Feel the relaxation in these muscles as the tension in the neck and shoulder muscles is released.

15. Focus on your face, cheeks, forehead, and throat. Contract your facial and throat muscles on inhalation. Deeply frown your forehead and grimace your mouth, bring the corners up toward your ears. Think of bitter squeezed lemon juice. Hold the position and feel the tension in your face.

16. On exhalation, relax the facial and neck muscles.

17. Review the state of relaxation of your body. Are there any areas that are tense or out of alignment? On inhalation, tense your body, hold the position for a few seconds and on exhalation, relax.

When you are ready to complete your relaxation exercise, open your eyes and gently stretch your whole body, and then slowly move to a sitting position. Allow yourself a few moments to become aware of your surroundings before getting up and continuing your daily activities.

Calming Your Mind and Your Breathing

There is a close relationship between the rhythm of your breathing and your intellectual, mental and emotional state. Short rapid breathing occurs when you are feeling tense from anxiety, fear, anger, or excitement. Simply by calming the breath, you will feel calmer in these other dimensions of your being. By calming your breathing, you break the cycle of these emotions and the mental blocks they cause. Breathing can be used on its own or as an accompaniment to either mental and/or muscle-focused relaxation.

1. Ensure that you are in a comfortable position, that your body is in alignment, and that your head is balanced. Close your eyes.
2. Focus on your breathing. Concentrate on how the breath flows in and out of your nose.
3. Inhale deeply and calmly, pause, and then exhale calmly, pause.
4. Do not force the breath. Notice how warm each out-breath is.
5. Imagine with each intake of breath, warm loving positive energy flows into you, gently recharging you.
6. With every out-breath, imagine all the tensions and worries you have leaving you.
7. Notice the feelings of heaviness in your head and your limbs with each exhalation.
8. If you feel pain in any part of your body, imagine the breath flowing over that part of your body and taking away the pain.
9. Become aware of each of your muscles and how they slowly relax.
10. Feel the full support of whatever you are resting on.
11. When you are ready to rejoin the world, make a slow stretch and slowly move to a new position. Allow yourself a few minutes before you get up and reconnect with the activities of your life.

Be careful not to hyperventilate—that is, breathing in and out too quickly—which can cause you to feel dizzy.

Relaxing Your Mind

Many of the physiological responses of fight-or-flight originate from our thoughts. When you calm and still your mind, your body also becomes calmer and more relaxed.

1. Ensure that you are in a comfortable position, with your body in alignment and your head balanced. Close your eyes.
2. Tune in to your breathing. Breathe in slowly and calmly, pause, breathe out slowly and calmly, pause. As you exhale, say to yourself *r-e-l-a-x* and feel yourself sinking into the supporting environment.
3. Follow your thoughts and let them go. Don't try to force them out but don't hold on to them either. Imagine them floating away.

4. Become aware of your feelings. Let them go.
5. Focus on your breathing and when your mind wanders away, gently bring it back to your breath.
6. Imagine a little ball of light moving up your right leg toward the bottom of your spine.
7. Now imagine another small ball of light moving up your left leg and becoming absorbed into one ball of light at your coccyx.
8. Slowly imagine the ball of light moving up your body.
9. Imagine it moving down your right arm to the tip of your fingers and then down the left and back again to your centre.
10. Refocus on your thoughts. Gently let them go and simply become aware of your breathing. With each exhalation, feel yourself become more and more relaxed.
11. At this point, you can choose a word—a mantra—to repeat silently to yourself. Choose a word that you feel comfortable with and that sounds soothing to you, such as *love, peace,* or *tranquillity.* Repeat the word gently to yourself. Or you could envisage a scene that you find very beautiful and soothing—a scene in which you would be very relaxed and inactive. Or imagine soothing sounds like a running stream, or the waves of the ocean gently rolling up the beach. Engage all your five senses. What do you see, hear, smell, feel, and taste?
12. If your mind wanders, gently bring it back to your breathing.
13. Feel yourself floating on a cloud of grace; know that you are safely secure and surrounded by love that flows over you and through you. Bask in this feeling of love and tranquillity.
14. When you are ready to rejoin the world, gently stretch, open your eyes, yawn, and slowly return to an active position.

By simply practicing any one or even a single element of the above methods every day, morning and evening, you will discover that you are less tense, that your mind is more focused, and that your emotions are calm and in balance. Your day-to-day breathing will also be greatly improved. You will feel more energetic and calm, and your whole outlook on life will be enhanced. With practice, you will be able to conduct these exercises in any situation, maintaining a relaxed and balanced state of mind no matter what the circumstances.

The Power of Music

Positively coping with stress takes time. Time is needed to unwind and relax and to act in a controlled and mature way. Try methods of relaxing and experiment with which one best work for you. Listening to music can be an effective way of relaxing and coping. Experiment with this as you complete your final activity for this chapter.

6.8 Activity: Assess the Impact of Music

Select four pieces of music that create different responses in you, such as feeling relaxed and at peace, angry and on edge, or bouncy and happy. Listen to each piece of music and do the following:

- Record how you feel and how this may reflect different aspects of your life.
- Record how you cope in these situations.
- Write about how each piece of music makes you think and behave.

Scheduling and Recording Daily Relaxation

A way of helping this become a regular habit is to schedule time in your day to relax. It seems ridiculous that we need to go to such lengths, but that is the reality of modern-day living. On an ongoing basis, record when you have practiced the exercises, which ones specifically helped you, and how you felt afterwards. This process will help you discover which methods suit you best and reinforce the benefit of the practice.

The combined weight of stressors and coping startegies, both negative and positive, will determine how effectively you are able to cope on a physical, emotional, mental and spiritual level. In turn, this will determine your position on the vital-energy continuum and the amount of vital energy you have available to you on a daily basis.

6.9 Activity: Grounding Exercises

The butterfly hug: Stand with your feet firmly pressed into the ground. Monitor your breathing and attain a sense of calm and peace and give yourself a big hug by wrapping both of your arms around yourself and then repeatedly and gently patting yourself on the back. This should feel quite comforting.

Safe place: In the second exercise, you can be comfortably seated or lying down. Choose an imaginary place where you will feel very safe and secure. It may be on top of a mountain, in a little stone cottage—or even in the Oval Office in the White House! Imagine your surroundings—what can you see, smell, hear, taste, and feel? Are there any other people with you? What time of day is it? What is the weather doing? What are you wearing, and what is the texture against your skin? Monitor your breathing and listen to your heart rate. Imagine them both slowing down. Do a body scan to identify where the tension is in your body. Imagine a spiral of energy around the tension and then imagine the spiral moving in the opposite direction. Breathe deeply and let it go. Give your safe place a name and remember that you can go there any time you want to.

Burnouts Are Caused by Reactions to Stress

Not successfully coping with stressors, even small everyday ones, slowly drains away your reserves, and over time you will suffer from burnout. Burnout occurs when we overdraw on our reserves to cope with stressors. Indicators of burnout are fatigue, headaches, muscular pain, deterioration in mental abilities, low self-esteem, a cynical, blaming attitude, poor interpersonal relationships, excessive negative coping behaviour (such as smoking or drinking), and a negative attitude to your work with a high incidence of absenteeism and/or changing jobs.

Burnout occurs when we overextend our reserves. At any one time, we have a limited amount of reserves. Our carrying capacity and the amount of reserves we have built up from accumulating eustress determine the limit. When the stress withdrawals exceed our carrying capacity and our eustress reserves, we start to move to the negative poles of the potential dimensions. If this withdrawal continues, we may find ourselves in the situation of exhaustion and, failing corrective action, a premature death. To simplify these relations, look at the following mathematical equation.

The Vital Energy Exchange Equation

+ / - Carrying capacity

+ / - Stressors

+ / - Coping behaviours

+ / - Environment

= Position on the vital energy continuum

= Amount of vital energy available for current and future adventures

6.10 Activity: Plot Your Vital Energy Co-ordinates

Plot your co-ordinates on the Vital Health Energy Health Continuum below. Then, in your journal, reflect on how healthy you are and what may be inhibiting you from reaching your full capacity and potential.

The Vital Energy Health Continuum Dimensions

	Minimum potential		Maximum potential
Cognitive ability	Unfocused	_____	Focuse
Physical health	Disease	_____	Ease
Emotional well-being	Unstable	_____	Stable
Social integration	Alienated	_____	Integrated
Spirituality awareness	Closed	_____	Enlightened
Environment	Unsupportive	_____	Supportive (safe)

Your free will and the ability to choose your thoughts and actions distinguishes you from other animals in that it allows you to adapt rapidly to different environments without having to follow the long and involved evolutionary processes of other species. Successful coping behaviours should accommodate all the systems in our lives.

Our behaviours either become generators of additional distress, as in the case of smoking or overeating, or generators of eustress. How successfully we manage our environment and ourselves determines how much energy and time we have to be productive, be successful, and live a meaningful life. It is all in our hands and in our thoughts. How we utilise our life-force energy is manifested in our day-to-day roles and how we fill our time.

6.11 Activity: Reflection

> Reflect in your journal on your findings so far. What is your physical, emotional and mental health? What is your social and environmental context like? Are there any changes that you would like to explore so as to enhance your carrying capacity?

An important component of remaining healthy and determining the amount of vital energy you have available for you to use is your nutritional intake. This topic is discussed in detail on the next leg of your journey.

CHAPTER 7
Galley—Healthy Eating

Tell me what you eat, and I will tell you who you are.

—Brillat-Savarin

The spirit cannot endure the body when overfed, but, if underfed, the body cannot endure the spirit.

—St Frances de Sales

The doctor of the future will give no medication, but will interest his patients in the care of the human frame, diet and in the cause and prevention of disease.

—Thomas A Edison

When walking, walk. When eating, eat.

—Rashaski · Zen Proverb

Itinerary

In this chapter, we will explore and develop a general understanding of how to plan meals so as to ensure that you have the ingredients required for a nutritionally balanced diet that will promote optimal health and maintain a healthy weight.

Viewpoint

- inductive and deductive reasoning
- nutrition

Travel Bag

You will need:
- your journal
- a calculator
- access to the Internet

Introduction

The content and quality of what we eat plays an important role in our emotional and physical well-being. The types of foods we eat can significantly impact, either positively or negatively, our energy levels, our moods, and our health, including our immune system. It is in being conscious of this impact and how foods are used by the body that you can plan a healthy menu and thereby improve the quality of your life.

Macronutrients in food are converted into energy through a number of complex processes. After food is digested, nutrients are absorbed into the bloodstream and transported to and absorbed within the cells of the body, where they are further metabolised into a form of chemical energy the body can use or store. This process requires oxygen and many cofactors and coenzymes.

To continue with the metaphor of transportation and travel, your body is like an engine that needs power for the movement, building and maintenance of your craft or vehicle. Most engines need a variety of substances to keep them running efficiently—for example, fuel, oil and water. The quantity of these will vary depending on the size, make, age and capacity of the vehicle. The volume of fuel required will also depend on the extent of engine usage—that is, how far the vehicle has to travel and at what speed. Similarly, your body requires a combination of different substances, depending on your age, sex, body type, and physical activity level. These fuels include carbohydrates, lipids (fats), proteins, water, vitamins, minerals, and phytochemicals.

7.1 Activity: Snapshot of Current Nutritional Intake

Before embarking on your nutritional journey, keep a food diary for a week, detailing the foods, snacks, and drinks you eat during that period. Reflect in your journal on what you consider to be a healthy diet.

Variety of Foods

Foods occur in great variety. In Western cultures, there has been a tendency to move toward more processed convenience foods.; however, globally, this is not always the case. Western processed foods tend to be energy-dense and nutrient-poor. Energy-dense foods provide a lot of kilojoules/calories in a small portion of food that is high in fat or sugar—for example, pastries, chocolate bars and soft drinks. Low-energy-dense foods that are low in kilojoules or calories are often high in fibre and water content, which provide volume and weight but not much in the way of energy. Typically these are vegetables, fruits and whole grains. Grapefruit, for example, is approximately 90 per cent water, and fresh raw carrots are about 88 per cent water.

Organic foods are foods that are grown as a natural whole system, without the use of synthetic chemicals like pesticides or artificial fertilisers. They are not genetically modified or exposed to radiation. See the following website for more information: http://www.ifoam.org/growing_organic/definitions/doa/index.html.

7.2 Activity: *What Do People Around the World Eat?*

Look up and watch the YouTube video "What Families Around the World Eat Each Week." In your journal, reflect on what you noticed with regards to quantity, variety, and sense of vitality of the families representing the different countries viewed. To what extent are these families eating processed as opposed to unprocessed food? Write in your journal how your diet reflects a particular eating style.

Energy Requirements

According to the National Health and Medical Research Council (NHMRC) website at http://www.nrv.gov.au/energy.htm, nutrients are converted into energy through the process of digestion. Energy is required in the body for metabolic processes, physiological functions, muscular activity, heat production, growth, and synthesis of new tissues. Your basal metabolic rate (BMR) is the energy that is required to maintain your regular bodily functions and your physiological processes. Your physical activity level (PAL) also affects your energy intake. Energy is released from food components by oxidation. The main sources of energy are carbohydrates, lipids (fats), proteins, and to a lesser degree, alcohol.

In Australia, nutritional information is presented in kilojoules, while in America it is presented in calories (also known as kilocalories). To convert calories to kilojoules, multiply calories by 4.18. For example:

1 cup of orange juice is 116 calories, which converts to
116 x 4.18   = 485 kilojoules

Conversely, to convert kilojoules to calories, divide the kilojoules by 4.18:
10 grams of carbohydrates   = 170 kilojoules of energy or 41 calories

When considering quantities of food, you also need to take into account the energy value of each food source.

Conversion of Macronutrients Food Source to Energy

Each of these food sources has a unique molecular structure, which provides the body with the components for healthy maintenance, functioning, and energy—except for alcohol, which is known as an empty food source, as it provides large amounts of kilojoules but *no* nutrients.

The estimated energy contribution from each of the following macronutrients is:

	Kilojoules/Gram	Calories/Gram
Carbohydrates	17	4
Lipids (fats)	37	9
Protein	17	4
Alcohol	29	7

Components of Different Food Sources

The digestion of food involves a variety of different physical and chemical processes:

- chewing
- enzymes in the mouth, stomach, and intestines
- bacteria living in the colon
- HCL and bile
- muscular action of the gut
- enzymes produced by bacteria living in the gut

Thereafter, the digested food is absorbed into the bloodstream and its various chemical components transported to wherever it is required by the cells of the body. The components required by the body in different proportions are:

- carbohydrates
- proteins
- lipids (fats)
- fluids
- fibre
- vitamins
- minerals
- phytochemicals

Summary of Recommended Food Sources

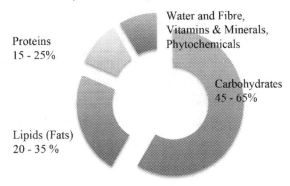

101

Carbohydrates

Carbohydrates are made up of carbon, hydrogen and oxygen. They include simple sugars like glucose, fructose and lactose, plus complex compounds like starch and dietary fibre. These simple to complex compounds, when digested and absorbed, provide the body with glucose. Some types of dietary fibre are used by bacteria within the gut to produce short-chain fatty acids, which are also absorbed and used to further maintain the body's internal cells.

Generally, natural (unprocessed) foods contain dietary fibre, vitamins, minerals and phytochemicals along with the carbohydrate. Processed foods, however, often contain carbohydrates in the form of added sugars with little or no fibre, vitamins, minerals, and phytochemicals. Carbohydrates found in natural (unprocessed) foods are more diverse and complex. In the refining process, the peel, bran and husks are often discarded, reducing the fibre content and the diversity of the carbohydrates present. Foods that are a good source of carbohydrate include grains, legumes, fruits and some vegetables. Milk and yoghurt provide lactose, which is a carbohydrate.

As carbohydrates are digested in the gut, glucose is absorbed into the bloodstream, which transports it around the body. Whitney et. al. (2011) suggest that within one to four hours after a meal, all of the sugars and most of the starches have been digested. Glucose that is not immediately required by the body for energy is stored as fat.

Proteins

Proteins are made up of amino acids in a variety of different compositions. Some of these are essential and have to be accessed through diet, as the body is unable to synthesise them sufficiently. Others are non-essential, as they can be produced within the body. Proteins play an important role in a number of bodily functions, including:

- creating enzymes that enable chemical reactions
- building cell-membrane structure
- carrying iron and oxygen
- maintaining water balance
- binding structures within the cell, for example DNA and RNA
- enabling movement in the muscles

Proteins within the body are continually replaced. For example, proteins used within the blood are generally replaced within two months, while proteins in the bones last about a year. When these proteins are replaced, the old proteins are broken down to their original amino acids and recycled in a pool of amino acids. Newly required body proteins are synthesised from this pool, which also contains amino acids derived from the diet. If the amino acids are not recycled continuously—for example, if they can't be reused and there is an excess of amino acids in the pool—these are further broken down and either stored as fat or broken down further and excreted.

If energy (glucose) is in short supply, protein can be harvested by the body as an energy supply. Amino acids are diverted to glucose rather than used to generate new or replacement proteins; in these circumstances, muscles and other tissues waste away.

Most foods we eat contain protein. Meat, fish, milk, legumes and eggs are good sources of high-quality protein, followed by grains and to a far lesser extent fruit and vegetables. It is recommended an adult have an intake of approximately 75 grams of protein a day; however, this is variable and will be affected by a number of factors, including age and physical activity. In order for the body to have access to all twenty essential amino acids, a varied diet is essential.

Fats (Lipids)

Fat is an excellent source of energy. Dietary fat is also needed to facilitate the absorption and transportation of fat-soluble vitamins, minerals and phytochemicals, many of which have a protective factor in the form of antioxidants. Fats that are processed often change in their physical, chemical, and biotechnological composition, and unsaturated fats often become saturated fats or trans fats. Processed fats are commonly saturated and are found in cakes, biscuits, snack foods, fast foods, meat, and dairy products. Most authorities recommend that we minimise the intake of saturated fats, as these have been linked to disease, particularly heart disease.

Fats are generally found in energy-dense foods. Energy-dense foods are foods that release high kilojoules/calories per gram, such as meat.

Fluid Intake Per Day

Water is essential to life. The body is made up of approximately 60 per cent water. It is essential that this fluid is replenished regularly so as to best facilitate the cooling of the body, the transportation of nutrients within the body and waste from it.

The ideal fluid intake is made up of the liquid that you drink plus that which is contained in the food that you eat. For more information, visit http://www.nrv.gov.au and select the "Calculator" tab.

Fibre Intake

Fibre is found in grains, fruits, and vegetables, and is—for humans—the non-digestible or digestion-resistant part of food. Diets that are rich in fibre are typically high in fruits, vegetables, legumes, and grains. Fibre is found to be more concentrated in the outer layers and peel of the plant food and not in highly processed food. For example, wholegrain bread is estimated to have 25 per cent more fibre than white bread.

The role of fibre in the digestive process is complex and dependent on multiple factors. It is believed that fibre's main role is to facilitate the movement of food through the digestive tract, the absorption and excretion of cholesterol, and the overall excretion process. It also acts as a food source for bacteria living in the gut, which play an important role in the digestive process. Meals high in fibre tend to create a full feeling for longer.

Researchers have found that fibre offers protection against diseases of affluence, such as heart disease, obesity and some cancers. These diseases are associated with diets high in processed and high-fat foods, low fibre intake and a lifestyle of low physical activity. Vegetables, fruit and unprocessed foods contribute to a high-fibre diet and help protect you against these diseases. For your dietary requirements of fibre, look at the following website: http://www.nrv.gov.au

Vitamins and Minerals

There are thirteen identified vitamins and twenty-two minerals that are found in small amounts in food. Each performs a single or number-specific function in the metabolic processes of the body. Similarly deficiencies and excesses in vitamins and minerals can lead to disease. These components, within a range of quantity, are essential to your health in order to allow the necessary maintenance and growth processes of the body. Estimated dietary requirements are detailed at http://www.nrv.gov.au.

Phytochemicals

Phytochemicals are found in all plant foods—such as fruits and vegetables, nuts, seeds, grains, legumes, herbs, and spices—and also in beverages like tea and coffee. There are over 12,000 identified phytochemicals that help strengthen the body and prevent disease. Extensive research has indicated that there is a strong correlation between the high consumption of fruits and vegetables and good health.

Many phytochemicals have antioxidant compounds that assist in the regulation and strengthening of the immune system. Research has indicated that they reduce cholesterol absorption in the intestines, leading to reduced coronary disease. A high level of antioxidants has also been linked to a reduction in the incidence of cancer. Foods high in phytochemicals include the following:

- beverages—tea (especially green tea), red wine
- fruits—apples, pineapples, oranges, apricots, dates, oranges, grapefruit, red grapes, peaches, sultanas, raisins, rock melon, tomatoes, capsicums, avocado, lychees, kiwifruit, lemons, passion fruit, pawpaw
- berries—cranberries, blackberries, raspberries, strawberries
- vegetables—carrots, pumpkin, red cabbage, eggplant, zucchini, gherkins
- oil—olive oil, flaxseed oil
- herbs and spices—turmeric, white pepper, nutmeg, oregano, thyme, rosemary, basil, cinnamon, parsley, mint
- seeds—caraway seeds, pumpkin seeds, linseed
- legumes—French beans, soya beans, peas, chickpeas

- leeks, onions, garlic
- brassica vegetables—broccoli, cabbage, kale, mustard, Brussels sprouts, cauliflower
- soy products
- root vegetables—artichokes, chicory root, potatoes
- leafy vegetables—lettuce, celery, spinach
- cereals—oats, maize, millet
- mushrooms
- honey
- olives

For more information, visit http://lpi.oregonstate.edu/infocenter/phytochemicals.html.

Food-Based Nutrition

Most food is made up of a combination of macronutrients: carbohydrates, lipids (fats), and proteins. The next consideration is to decide how much of each macronutrient to eat. The acceptable macronutrient distribution range (AMDR) recommended by the National Health and Medical Research Council (NHMRC) suggests the following energy-consumption proportion for each macronutrient:

Macronutrient	% of total energy
Carbohydrates	45–65
Lipids	20–35
Proteins	15–25

Simplistic Summary of the Digestive and Absorption Process

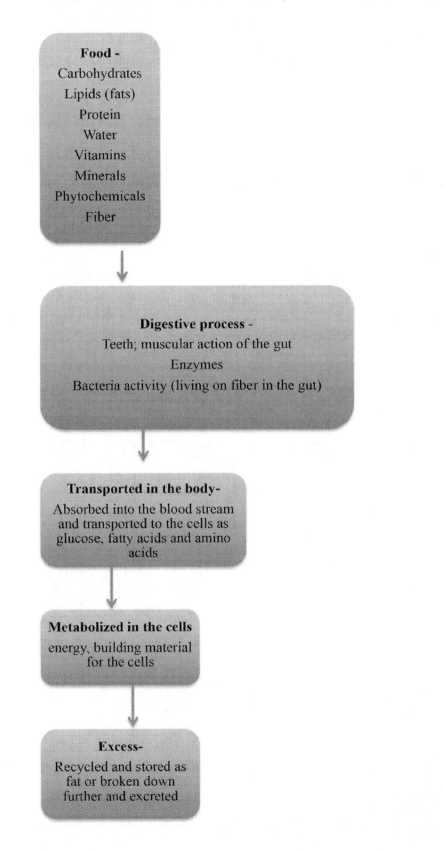

Food -
Carbohydrates
Lipids (fats)
Protein
Water
Vitamins
Minerals
Phytochemicals
Fiber

Digestive process -
Teeth; muscular action of the gut
Enzymes
Bacteria activity (living on fiber in the gut)

Transported in the body-
Absorbed into the blood stream and transported to the cells as glucose, fatty acids and amino acids

Metabolized in the cells
energy, building material for the cells

Excess-
Recycled and stored as fat or broken down further and excreted

Research on How Diet Impacts Our Health and Morbidity

Professor Ancel Keys initiated a longitudinal research project studying the diets of seven different countries, involving 12,000 male participants, with a thirty-year mortality follow-up. He found that the Mediterranean diet typical of the 1960s was significantly healthier than other traditional diets researched over the same period. Further analysis showed there was a link between high intake of fruits and vegetables and a decrease in stomach cancer; there was an increase in stomach cancer with a high intake of refined grains, but not whole grains and cereals (Willet et. al. 1995 as cited in Wahlqvist 2002).

The typical Mediterranean Greek diet of the 1960s had the following characteristics:

- high in unsaturated fat (mainly virgin olive oil, approximately four tablespoons a day, nearly always used to prepare vegetables and legumes, which helps the absorption of nutritional components in the intestines)
- high in low-energy-dense plant foods
- low in animal and saturated fats
- red/white meat, 35 grams a day
- cheese/yoghurts, 0–1 servings
- low intake of butter
- animals not grain-fed but grazed on wild natural vegetation and herbs
- high in nuts, wild greens, and legumes.
- low in carbohydrates, mainly low GI
- large amounts of vegetables (2–3 cups a day, approximately 350 grams), generally of the dark green leafy type, including endive, chicory, amaranth, and spinach; often served in soups and casseroles, thereby retaining nutrients that would otherwise have been leached out during the cooking process
- legumes, 30 grams a day
- nuts, 30 grams a day
- fruit, 450 grams, or two to three pieces of fruit, a day
- Wholegrain cereals, 450 grams (for example, 6 to 8 slices of bread) a day
- Fish, 40 grams a day
- Alcohol, 20 grams (two standard drinks) a day

This research has been supported by the Lyon Heart Study (sample size of 600) that linked diet to heart disease. People who had survived a heart attack were divided into two groups and given either the Mediterranean diet or the diet recommended by the American Heart Association. After a four-year period, the results showed that the participants who followed a Mediterranean diet showed a 70 per cent reduction in all causes of mortality compared to similar sufferers who followed the diet recommended by the American Heart Association (De Lorgeril et al. 1998 as cited in Wahlqvist (2002)).

In another study, conducted by Ortega (1997), the results indicated that a diet with a high intake of fruit and vegetables and therefore high in minerals, vitamins, and phytochemicals, positively correlated with better memory performance in people sixty-five and older.

Certain fatty acids are particularly involved in the function of the brain and the immune system and play a role in limiting inflammation. In a multinational diet comparison, a strong correlation was found between high fish consumption and low levels of depression (Hibbelen 1998, as cited in Wahlqvist (2002)).

Research has indicated that the more varied the diet, the healthier. The intake of a variety of foods increases the chances of gaining a more diverse range of minerals, vitamins, and important phytochemicals. Research further suggests that a minimum portion size of two tablespoons of thirty classes of different foods, including herbs and spices, over a one-week period will ensure an adequate nutrient intake.

To increase variety, it is suggested that one purchase foods that contain a range of nutritional ingredients, for example wholemeal breads. Ideally, meals should comprise small portions with many different ingredients. Below is a list of fifty-seven food items from which it is recommended to select thirty classes of food during a one-week period. (Savige et al. 1997, as cited in Wahlqvist 2002, 552–553.)

Weekly Food Variety Checklist

1. Eggs (any variety)

Dairy
2. Milk, ice cream, cheese, yoghurt (without live cultures)

Live cultures
3. Yoghurt (with live culture, e.g. acidophilus, bifidobacteria)

Yeast
4. Vegemite

Fish (including canned)
5. Fatty fish (tuna, anchovies, salmon, kipper, sardines, herring, mackerel, pilchards)
6. Fish (saltwater)
7. Fish (freshwater)
8. Roe (caviar, taramasalata)
9. Shellfish and molluscs (muscles, oysters, squid, scallops)
10. Crustaceans (prawns, lobsters, crabs, shrimps)

Meat
11. Lamb, beef, veal
12. Pork (including ham and bacon)

13. Poultry (chicken, duck, turkey)
14. Game (quail, wild duck, pigeon)
15. Game (kangaroo, rabbit)
16. Liver
17. Brains
18. All other organ meats

Legumes (including canned)

19. Peas (fresh, dried, split peas), chickpeas (dried, roasted), beans (haricot, kidney, lima, broad), lentils (red, brown, green), soy products (tofu, milk), peanuts, peanut butter

Cereals

20. Wheat (bread, pasta, ready-to-eat)
21. Corn (including ready-to-eat)
22. Barley (including ready-to-eat)
23. Oats (including ready-to-eat)
24. Rye (including ready-to-eat)
25. Rice (including ready-to-eat)
26. Other grains and cereals (buckwheat, millet, quinoa, sago, semolina, tapioca, triticale)

Fats and oils

27. Oils
28. Hard/soft spreads

Beverages

29. Water (and mineral)
30. Non-alcoholic (tea, coffee, cocoa)
31. Alcohol (wine, beer, spirits)

Fermented foods

32. Miso, tempeh, soy sauce
33. Sauerkraut
34. All other variety

Sugar confectionary

35. All varieties (plus soft drinks)

Vegetables (including canned and frozen)

36. Root and tubers (potato, carrot, sweet potatoes, beetroot, parsnip, bamboo shoots, ginger, radish, water chestnut)
37. Flowers (broccoli, cauliflower)
38. Stalks (celery, asparagus)

39. Onion (spring onion, leeks, garlic)
40. Tomatoes, okra
41. Beans (green, snow peas)
42. Leafy greens (spinach, cabbage, silver beet, endive, kale, chicory, parsley, lettuce)
43. Peppers (capsicum, chillies)
44. Marrow-like (zucchini, squash, cucumber, turnips, eggplants, swede)
45. Fungi (mushrooms)
46. Herbs/spices

Nuts and seeds

47. Almond, cashew, chestnut, coconut, hazelnut, pecan, pine nut, pistachio, walnut, pumpkin seed, flaxseed, sesame seed, tahini, hummus, sunflower seed

Fruit

48. Stone (nectarines, peaches, cherries, plums, apricots, avocados, olives, prunes)
49. Apples
50. Pears, nashi
51. Berries (raspberries, strawberries)
52. Grapes (raisins, sultanas)
53. Bananas
54. Citrus (orange and lemon)
55. Melon (honeydew, watermelon)
56. Kiwi, date, passion fruit
57. Tropical (mango, pineapple, guava, jackfruit, lychee, papaya, star fruit)

Notes
- *Grains and cereals:* Wheat includes wholemeal, ready-to eat cereals like Weetabix, bran flakes.
- *Serving size:* Quantities smaller than 1 to 2 tablespoons (except for fats, oil, Vegemite, chillies, herbs, spices) would not be eaten in sufficient quantity to rate as a serving—for example, a slice of tomato on a hamburger is less than two tablespoons and therefore does not constitute a serving.

A purist would argue that alcohol, and confectionary should not be included in the above list!

7.3 Activity: Complete the Above Checklist.

Referring back to Activity 7.1, evaluate how comprehensive your diet was over the one-week period. Score 1 point for each food category eaten. The maximum score for this checklist is 57. A score of 30 or more indicates an adequately varied diet. Reflect in your journal on any deficiencies that you have noticed and any changes that you are considering making to your diet.

Guidelines for Planning a Healthy Menu

The following guidelines can help you in your attempt to change your daily nutrition for the better.

- Eat wholefoods. These are foods in their whole, natural state with a minimum of additives, processing, and packaging. This reduces the number of preservatives and additives that can be harmful. It also increases the fibre available in your system and so improves the digestive process. Processed foods, on the other hand, are often energy-dense but nutrient-poor and low in phytochemicals. Sometimes processed foods may not be energy-dense, but contain many additives to provide the taste of fat or the sweetness of sugar.
- Eat a variety of foods, both in source and colour. This increases the chances of obtaining the necessary vitamins, minerals and phytochemicals required.
- Prepare foods in a variety of different ways. Some nutrients are available only from raw foods and others only from cooked foods. So preparation is a further factor that helps increase the availability of different nutrients required by the body.
- Eat fresh food for improved quality and therefore availability of nutrients.
- Adapt traditional recipes by adding lots of different foods to increase variety—including onions, garlic, parsley, spices, vegetables, and herbs.
- Increase protective foods high in antioxidants, including fish, garlic, onions, deeply coloured vegetables, soy, tomatoes, apples, citrus fruits, grapes, berries, olives, and herbal teas.
- Eat foods from different cultures. Again, this increases variety.
- Sprinkle small amounts of salt. There is evidence that some people who consume excessive salt over a number of years experience hypertension.
- Use a variety of liquid plant fats, such as coconut milk and extra virgin olive oil. Unsaturated fat (good fat) is found in olive oil or canola oil. Extra virgin olive oil is high in antioxidants and light in added chemicals. Canola oil has been found to have more unsaturated fats vs. saturated fats than olive oil, but fewer phytochemicals.
- Use a variety of low-energy-density foods, such as tofu, Asian leafy greens, and tomatoes.
- At least twice a week, eat a portion of fresh or tinned fish.
- Include at least one or two legumes per week in place of meat to reduce animal fats and increase fibre—for example, tofu or baked beans.
- Include a handful of a variety of nuts several times a week to increase intake of unsaturated fats.
- Include egg dishes weekly in place of meat dishes.
- Include several servings daily of reduced-fat high-calcium milk and milk products, or calcium-fortified soymilk or tofu to ensure sufficient calcium intake.

- Try to have several cups of a variety of vegetables per day, especially dark green leafy types and deep-coloured vegetables, as these are rich in phytochemicals, vitamins, minerals, and fibre.
- Try to have at least two pieces of fruit daily, especially apples, citrus, grapes and berries.
- Choose lean meats and reduced-fat alternatives in dairy products and processed foods, to limit the intake of domestic animal fats.
- Choose kangaroo and/or pasture-fed rather than grain-fed beef,
- Choose unrefined natural fats found in nuts, seeds, fish, soy, olives and avocado, as these foods include other valuable nutrients and phytochemicals.
- Choose foods that are low-GI. Foods with a high GI do not necessarily have any immediate effect, but long-term consumption of foods with a high GI is believed to be associated with an increased risk of inflammation.
- Use cold-pressed monounsaturated oil (between one to three tablespoons a day) for cooking vegetables, legumes, and fish dishes, as it improves the taste and helps with the absorption of fat-soluble vitamins and phytochemicals from plant foods. These are high in unsaturated fats.
- Marinate meat and fish in wine, lemon juice, herbs, spices and extra virgin olive oil to increase the variety and flavour.
- Serve herbs, spices, and chutney with a meal to enhance the flavour of dishes.
- Increase daily consumption of water and tea to increase fluid intake. Phytochemicals occur in teas.
- Limit fruit juice to less than two small glasses per day because of the high sugar content. High refined-sugar consumption has been linked to tooth decay, gum disease and unhealthy blood-sugar spikes.
- Avoid salted, cured, smoked, or pickled foods, as these have been found to increase the risk of colorectal cancer.
- Limit your intake of red meat, and eat lean red meat to avoid intake of animal fats.
- Limit intake of processed foods and sauces, as they often have high levels of sugar and the fats tend to be denatured.
- Limit intake of processed sugar, replacing it with, for example, cinnamon or honey.
- Avoid nutrient-empty foods like alcohol. Alcohol provides a high level of energy (27 kilojoules per gram), but it is generally nutrient-poor. Excessive alcohol consumption leads to cognitive detrition and abdominal obesity, which is a health risk.
- Avoid a high consumption of caffeine—for example, coffee, tea and caffeinated soft drinks.
- In general, minimize the food's exposure to excessive heat, as this denatures the quality of the nutrients
- Use healthy cooking methods. Avoid deep-frying, charring foods, overcooking meat, burning meat juices, and pan-frying.
- Cook using low temperatures: steaming, boiling, poaching, stewing, braising, stir-frying.

- Cook and serve foods in their juices—for example, in soups and casseroles. This helps to retain all the nutrients.
- We are conditioned to eat a certain quantity of food per serving. If you want to lose weight but eat the same-sized meals, eat low-energy-density foods like vegetables, using meat as a condiment. Meals high in fibre create a sense of fullness for longer.
- Healthy eating (according to holistic nutrition principles) aims to optimise beneficial substances, such as nutrients and phytochemicals, whilst minimising exposure to potentially harmful substances, such as contaminants.

Other suggestions are available at the Eat for Health website http://www.eatforhealth.gov.au.

7.4 Activity: Visit an Organic Market and a Fast-Food Outlet

Take yourself off to one of your local organic food markets. They usual occur weekly or monthly in a public place. Have a wander around and get a sense of the atmosphere and the people you meet in the stores and shopping there. Then visit a fast-food outlet and note what you experience of the people working in and accessing food from that service. What do you notice that specifically strikes you?

7.5 Activity: Plan a Menu for a Week

Reflect in your journal on any insights you have had as a consequence of this process.

Reading Food Labels

Each country has its own requirements with respect to the content and ingredients used in the processing of foodstuffs. This includes the name of the food, percentage of ingredients used, use-by date, nutrition information, additives, manufacturer details, directions on how to store the food, and on occasion nutritional claims like "cholesterol free." The information provides consumers with nutritional information that enables them to make an informed decision about the foods they purchase. It also allows the consumer to calculate the kilojoule or calorie value of portions served.

All this information is available from the app myfittnesspal; for more information, visit http://www.myfitnesspal.com.

Healthy Weight

To maintain a healthy weight, nutritional intake (energy) must balance energy expenditure. If your food and beverage consumption brings in more energy than you expend through activity, you will put on weight. Similarly, if you take in less than you use, you will lose weight. The amount of energy required will vary depending on your age, gender, sex, body size and shape, and physical activity level (PAL).

Nutritionists suggest gradual weight-loss goals combined with a diet that meets your nutritional requirements. The best type of diet to help with weight management emphasises foods that are nutrient-dense, high in fibre, low-GI, low in fat, and with adequate good-quality protein. Very low-calorie diets can result in malnourishment. It is best to develop long-term healthy eating patterns and create eating and lifestyle patterns that are sustainable in the long term.

Despite a lot of research in the area of weight loss, there is still more that is unknown than is known. The body-mass index (BMI) gives an evaluation of your weight in terms of recommendations from the World Health Organization (WHO). It also gives an indication of a healthy weight range for you. For example, a female with a height of 161 centimetres and weight of 64 kilograms has a BMI of 24.7. This person is within the normal weight range, though at the upper end, as indicated on the table below.

BMI Range
Underweight = <18.5
Normal weight = 18.5–24.9
Overweight = 25–29.9
Obese = >30

The classification adopted by the WHO (for example, that a BMI below 18.5 is classified as underweight) is based on international standards developed for adults of European descent.

To calculate your BMI, look at the following website: http://www.health.gov.au/internet/healthyactive/publishing.nsf/Content/your-bmi.

BMI is useful, but it has limitations because it does not tell us about body composition, such as body-fat percentage. There are also some groups in the population for whom BMI is not so useful and more sophisticated anthropometric measures are better. For more information, go to http://www.measureup.gov.au/internet/abhi/publishing.nsf/Content/Body%20Mass%20Index-lp.

Measuring waist circumference helps to overcome some of the limitations of BMI. The following website gives an indication of a person's health risk based on their waist circumference: http://www.measureup.gov.au/internet/abhi/publishing.nsf/Content/How+do+I+measure+myself-lp.

7.6 Activity: Consider you weight

Calculate your body mass index (BMI) and note your "ideal" weight range. Reflect in your journal how your current weight measures up to the World Health Organisation's recommended ideal healthy weight range for people of European descent.

Consult the Experts

A healthy diet and weight contribute significantly to an individual's physical mobility, mental alertness, and cognitive functioning, and this becomes increasingly obvious with age. Contact your GP for a referral to a dietician—or for a holistic approach, see a nutritionist or naturopath—if you feel that you need additional support in attaining a healthy diet and weight.

A nutritionist uses a combination of anthropometric measures, comprehensive questions and answers about health and lifestyle, dietary analysis, physical examinations, and laboratory tests in order to determine nutritional status and make recommendations for an individual. The information is viewed together in its entirety. Biochemical individuality is one of the key concepts underpinning nutrition, which is why there is no one perfect diet that suits everybody. Different people do well on different diets at different times in their lives.

If you would like to explore your diet further, look at the dietary analysis software available at FoodChoices, www.foodchoices.com.au.

Benefits

The benefits of healthy eating are far-reaching and greatly impact on our quality of life, both in our current day-to-day living and health and in the long term. This is affected by the quality of the food, which determines the amount of energy available for mental and physical activity. Eating regular nutritious meals can help to reduce cravings and mood swings as well as cardiovascular risk factors like high cholesterol and high blood pressure. In time, this leads to a correct healthy body weight.

 7.7 Activity: Mindfulness Exercise

Take a raisin and a lolly or sweet. Experience both. What is the texture of each, the smell and feel of them? Place one of them in your mouth at a time, and again experience the texture, taste, and overall sensation of the food item. Is there an aftertaste? Which provides a wholesome experience? A sense of satisfaction?

7.8 Activity: Reflection

In your journal, identify three changes that you are considering making to your eating habits—for example, how you shop for and prepare food. You may consider growing your own food. You could try your hand at growing your own sprouts, spinach, or lettuce.

This chapter has focused on assisting you in creating and maintaining a healthy physical environment. On the next leg of your journey, you will have the opportunity to consider the travellers you encounter in your social environment and how to best engage and connect with them so as to create a healthy and productive living and working context.

CHAPTER 8

Signals: The Gentle Art of Imparting

When Someone Deeply Listens to You

When someone deeply listens to you,
It is like holding out a dented cup that you've had since childhood
Watching it fill up with fresh, cold water.
When it balances on top of the brim, you are understood.
When it overflows and touches your skin, you are loved.
When someone deeply listens to you,
The room where you stay starts a new life,
The place where you wrote your first poem begins to glow in your
mind's eye.
It is as if gold has been discovered!
When someone deeply listens to you,
Your bare feet are on the earth, and a beloved land that seemed
distant
Is now home within you.
When someone deeply listens to you.

—John Fox

Itinerary

In this chapter, you will explore the characteristics that make you and others good communicators or imparters of information and be able to limit interference when sharing information.

Viewpoints

The focus will be on:
- communication
- interpersonal skills
- sense of self
- social awareness

Travel Bag

You will need:
- travelling companions
- your journal

Introduction

In this leg of the journey, you will be encouraged to rediscover the gentle art of imparting and sharing information. I've chosen the word *imparting* on purpose, as the term *communication* is so overused as to have lost its value. Imparting gives a deeper meaning and resonance to the concepts we are going to explore.

The letters from the word *imparting* can also form the words "I'm parting." That is, I am parting with something that is truly reflective of me, of who I am and what I value. It implies the potential to be open to the new and contradictory. That is true communication. Everything else is either filling in time, playing a game, or something implicitly more sinister in nature, *manipulation*.

In contemplating the presentation of this material, I recalled an acoustics exhibit at Singapore airport. The room was full of fun science activities to entertain children (and tempt adults) who were waiting for connecting flights. One of the exhibits included two huge concave discs approximately two metres in diameter placed opposite each other, about twenty metres apart, as illustrated below.

Imagine a space of twenty metres.

The activity required two participants to stand on a slightly raised platform, their backs to one another, and speak into the disc they were facing. The smooth concave design of the disc captured perfectly the person's message and rebounded it across the room to the other disc. The second person was able to hear a clear and undistorted message in spite of the activities and people in the space between the two discs.

Why did this experiment work so effectively? The mechanics are extremely simple. First, the discs are perfectly concave and have a smooth unblemished surface. Second, they are perfectly poised and completely dedicated to the art of sending and receiving information. Finally, they allow the transmission of one message, in one direction, at one time. If both people talk simultaneously, the content becomes confused and blurred. These simple communication principles also apply to human interaction.

Let us explore the qualities of the dish within the theme of our journey and see how we can emulate its effectiveness. The more we are able to take on the form of a concave disc when transmitting and receiving information, the more we will hear—in the deepest meaning of the word.

Your Craft: The Sender and Receiver

An important attribute of effective imparting is your level of self-esteem and self-attunement and how you choose to view a situation. Your self-esteem colours all that you see, hear, and do. It affects how you send your message and how you evaluate and interpret what you hear in return.

Listening entails neutralising yourself so that you can be open to the entire incoming message. This requires awareness of your emotions and the ability to put aside your values, beliefs, and potential judgments—to smooth your disc and make yourself as receptive as possible. This level of self-awareness demands an ability to observe yourself from two perspectives. The first perspective is from your crow's nest, a subjective view of what you feel, believe, and value. The second perspective is an objective view, which you can only achieve by moving outside of yourself. It means taking a dinghy and rowing away from your craft to a neutral position, like a mooring platform or buoy. From this perspective, you can start to view yourself objectively.

So how does your vessel look in relation to others? How are you lying in the water? Taking an objective view of yourself takes courage, persistence, and most importantly, tolerance and acceptance. It also puts you in a better position to view the other parties in an objective and neutral fashion.

Genuine Listening

Genuine listening means focusing on the full meaning of what the other person is saying. Understanding is found in interpreting the content within the frame of the sender's references, value system, needs, and situation. It includes hearing the timbre of the voice, the resonance of the core of the person's being, and what is being expressed.

To achieve this level of listening, you need to focus and put all your impulses and urges on hold. Ignore all distracting noises, particularly your internal urge to judge and prepare your reply. As a true listener, you need to empty yourself. Only after the other person has finished speaking and pauses can you reflect on and assimilate the content and consider your response.

This requires a time gap—the same gap that occurs between transmission of messages when speaking via the two discs in the science exhibition hall. The gap must be long enough to let you know that the other person has said all that he or she wants to say and for you to formulate and deliver an appropriate response. This is the meditative gap that allows us to stay in touch with who we are at our deepest level at any time. As a true listener, it is only when you have absorbed the total content of what has been said that you respond.

An empathic listener literally tries to put him- or herself in the other person's shoes, trying to understand that individual's perspective and outlook on life and the situation under discussion. This allows connection at the deepest possible level with the other person. Such integrity in communication allows for and is the foundation of intimacy, the highest and most valuable relationship with another human being.

For many, there is no need for a response—and so it is that still waters run deep!

The Other Craft: The Intended Recipient

In an ideal world, our travelling companion—the receiver—is a perfect replica of us, like the disc in the experiment (that is one reason it worked so well). The ideal receiver will understand every resonance of our being. But this is not an ideal world, and the reality is that everyone out there is different, has a different craft design and all the idiosyncrasies that make him or her unique.

Before considering the content of your message and medium and how you will send it, you need to give careful consideration to the nature of the recipient. It is now time to use your telescope or, if you are manning a more sophisticated craft, your radar. Consider what your receivers look like:

- What is the nature of their vessel, or is there a fleet of vessels?
- What is the appearance of the receivers? What are their clothes and how do they wear them? How is their health and grooming?
- What is their speech like?
- What are their needs, motives, and values?
- What is their level of self-esteem?
- What makes them sail out of the harbour?
- Are they givers or takers?
- Do they want to dominate and control, or are they free spirits?
- Who do they hang out with and why?
- What is the image they like to project?
- What are their successes and their failures?
- How do they cope with these?
- What are their hopes and fears?

All of these pointers help you to start to truly see your audience. Make your assessment and observation over a number of encounters—we all have an off day!

In keeping with our craft analogy, let's consider a couple of the characters that you probably encounter on a daily basis. A *battleship*, with its huge and intimidating artillery, is overly focused on receiving and interpreting every possible message and is always on the ready to interpret the message as a possible expression of aggression. A *windsurfer*, on the other hand, is youthful and free, with few encumbrances, happily and gaily abandoning himself or herself to the elements.

8.1 Activity: Draw a Vessel for People You Know Well

In your journal, draw and label a vessel for four of your close associates. Ideally, choose people with whom you have different quality relationships. You will build on this in your next activity, where you will consider your visibility and transparency to others.

Your Visibility on the Horizon

The more visible and transparent our motives, needs, and expectations, the more likely it is that the receiving party will understand our position, and the less chance there is for confusion and delivery of mixed messages. *Transparency* means allowing light to pass through, so that bodies can be seen distinctly. In the realm of physics, transparency is the transmitting of heat or other electromagnetic rays without distortion. In the realm of human interpersonal relations, it means the free flow of energy between people.

The Johari window model (Luft 1982) cleverly explains the dynamics of the concept of transparency. Two psychologists, Joseph Luft and Harry Ingram, developed the Johari window for the purpose of explaining the dynamics of growth to training groups. It is a useful tool in understanding the concept of energy flow from the perspective of giving and receiving information. If this is done effectively, it allows for more transparency in one's interpersonal relations. They proposed that we are made up of the combination of things that we know about ourselves and the things that other people know about us, as shown in the illustration.

Johari Window Model

	What I know about myself	What I do not know about myself
What others know	Arena	Blind spot
What others do not know	Façade	Unknown

Panes of the Johari Window

There are four panes a person has:

- arena
- facade
- blind spot
- unknown

Arena is the common area that we and others know about ourselves. An arena is the central part of an amphitheatre, theatre, or stadium. It is our public area, including such things as our race, sex, language and name. The arena represents the free flow of energy between others and ourselves.

Façade is the part of ourselves that we hide or think we hide from others. We present what we believe to be a fixed outward appearance, a shell or veneer that conceals who we are. Our racial prejudices may be something that we choose to hide behind a facade of neutrality or racial tolerance. We consciously block energy about ourselves to the outside world. This constant blocking and self-monitoring to ensure we are revealing only a small part of ourselves can be very draining on our vital energy reserves.

Blind spot refers to a side of us that is known to others and unknown to ourselves. The term derives from the anatomy of the eye, where at the point of entry/exit of the optic nerve, the retina is insensitive to light, and we are effectively blind in that spot. In the blind spot are behaviours about which we are totally ignorant, but which tell other people a great deal about us. For example, when a child is tired, she may twirl her hair and suck her thumb, unconscious of the message that she is sending.

Unknown is the part unknown to both the individual and the outside world, the part that is unexplored and uncharted. It may include early childhood experiences long since forgotten, or unrecognised abilities and weaknesses that have not yet had the opportunity to be revealed through life experiences—for example, the boundless love and exasperation that one experiences as a parent, or the courage one may find when facing a life-threatening disease. These mysterious parts of ourselves are difficult to reach with the conscious mind. Forgotten memories and past experiences can still have a powerful effect on our behaviour and emotions. It is through being open to others and life's experiences that we discover and expand this dimension of ourselves.

The dimensions of each pane of the Johari window are dynamic and change from day to day and from situation to situation. The breadth and depth of the arena is dependent on the extent to which a person is prepared to reveal himself or herself and on the extent to which a person is prepared to solicit information about himself or herself from others. Soliciting information includes seeking and receiving verbal, nonverbal and subliminal messages.

Increasing the Size of the Arena

When you actively ask for and give feedback, your arena grows, as does your self-knowledge, reducing your blind spot, façade and the unknown.

Johari Window Model: Tall Ship—Expanding Our Arena

	What I know about myself	What I do **not** know
	Ask for information	
Gives information What others know	*Large arena*	*Smaller blind spot*
What others do not know	*Smaller façade*	*Smaller unknown*

Ideally, there should be a balance between giving and receiving information.

Johari Window Model: Fishing Trawler

	What I know about myself	What I do **not** know
Asks for lots of information		
Gives very little information	Arena	Blind spot
What others know		
What others do not know	*Large Façade*	*Large Unknown*

Simply listening and asking for another's opinion tends to cause distrust, as the person giving information begins to grow suspicious of the questioner's motives and wonders if he or she is being manipulated. I have called this window configuration the fishing trawler.

Johari Window Model: Jet Ski

	What I know	What I do **not** know about myself
Gives a lot of information		
What others know	Arena	*Large blind spot*
What others do not Know	Façade	*Large unknown*

The converse, always telling and never listening, creates an impression of extreme egocentrism, and this too destroys any relationship. I have termed this approach the jet ski. This person is a highly motivated, energetic and "successful" up-and-coming executive, moving so fast that he or she hardly has time to position the disc. More than likely, your words will land only in his or her wake.

Johari Window Model: Submarine

What I know about myself   What I do not know
                                  about myself

Seeks and gives very little information

What others know   Arena   *Large
                                         Blind Spot*

What others do   *Large   *Large
not know   Façade*   Unknown*

Finally, people who neither give nor receive information have a small arena and a reduced energy flow. Over time, due to their lack of participation, they are excluded and become isolated from the energy input of others. They often become stagnant. Maintaining a high level of withdrawal is personally energy-consuming. I have called this person the submarine. A submarine is typically closed and secretive, only occasionally risking raising his or her periscope. No suggestion of a receptive disc or even a glimpse of the actual vessel!

Each configuration may be appropriate at a certain time, place and situation. The secret lies in consciously choosing that which is appropriate and being aware of the potential restrictions of energy flow and the effect on the quality of the imparting as a consequence of your and the other person's chosen frame of reference.

Let's revisit your craft and consider how transparent or visible you are with four of your current travelling companions.

8.2 Activity: Determine Your Visibility Rating

Ideally, choose the following four people: an immediate member of your family, a work or student colleague, a close female friend, and a close male friend. From the personal characteristics considered so far, consider how transparent or visible you are to them. Complete the matrix on the following pages. After completing the matrix, note where there are gaps. What can you learn from this?

Visibility Rating Matrix

Please note: this has been adapted from Bienvenu's Interpersonal Communication Inventory (1971).

Part A: For each of the following qualities, consider the extent to which you share yourself with others on a scale of 0 to 4, with 0 indicating that you do not share anything and 4 reflecting that you share everything with that person.

What I Share With Other People

Possible qualities	Name	Name	Name	Name	Total
1. Skills and knowledge					
2. Beauty					
3. Problems					
4. Tangible results					
5. Standard of living					
6. Creative					
7. Freedom					
8. Conservation					
9. Personal development					
10. Finances					
11. Authority					
12. Changes					
13. Environment					

Possible qualities	Name	Name	Name	Name	Total
14. Leadership					
15. Relationships					
16. Society					
17. Status					
18. Pleasure					
19 Leisure					
20. Responsibility					
21. Religious principles					
22. Variety					
23. Recognition					
24. Community					
25. Attitude					
26. Racial preference					
27. Travel					
28. Personal growth					
29. Physical health					
30. Sex life					
31. Hobbies					
32. Long-term plans					
33. Politics					
34. Privacy					
35. Appearance					
36. Parenting					

Possible qualities	Name	Name	Name	Name	Total
37. Culture					
38. Risk-taking					
39. Education					
40. Human rights					
Total					

Part B: Consider the extent to which others share the following qualities with you on a scale of 0 to 4, with 0 representing none and 4 that they share everything.

What Other People Share With Me

	Name	Name	Name	Name	Total
1. Skills and knowledge					
2. Beauty					
3. Problems					
4. Tangible results					
5. Standard of living					
6. Creative					
7. Freedom					
8. Conservation					
9. Personal development					
10. Finances					
11. Authority					
12. Changes					
13. Environment					

	Name	Name	Name	Name	Total
14. Leadership					
15. Relationships					
16. Society					
17. Status					
18. Pleasure					
19. Leisure					
20. Responsibility					
21. Religious principles					
22. Variety					
23. Recognition					
24. Community					
25. Attitude					
26. Racial preference					
27. Travel					
28. Personal growth					
29. Physical health					
30. Sex life					
31. Hobbies					
32. Long-term plans					
33. Politics					
34. Privacy					
35. Appearance					
36. Parenting					

	Name	Name	Name	Name	Total
37. Culture					
38. Risk taking					
39. Education					
40. Human rights					
Total					
Total from Part A					
Grand Total					

I once gave this exercise to a young work colleague. She was involved in a rather turbulent relationship with a younger man employed by the same company in a junior position. They were living together and had a six-month-old baby. They were financially strapped. Not an ideal situation! On completing the matrix, she was stunned to discover how little she had shared of herself with her partner. On asking herself why, she recognised an enormous fear. She was afraid that if he really knew her, he might reject and abandon her and take their child.

This was her third child. Her first husband had absconded to another continent with her first two children. At the time, she did not have the resources to follow and find them and five years had now passed since she had last seen them. Her fear was based within the reality of a previous experience. By reviewing the matrix, she realised that much of the conflict in her present relationship was a consequence of not trusting and sharing herself with her new partner. Once she understood this, she found the courage to share more of herself and took the risk of changing her superficial relationship into a deeper, more intimate one. They were married eight months later, and though they still have their difficult moments, her insight and consequent actions improved and enriched their relationship enormously.

Transparency is achieved by asking probing questions and absorbing verbal and nonverbal cues; by being clear and distinct in one's opinions, beliefs and behaviours; and by taking ownership of them. It also entails recognising and allowing others to choose and own their opinions, beliefs, and behaviours.

Your degree of transparency is determined in part by what you say and do not say, but it is also presented subtly by body language and your sense of personal space.

The Nature of the Other Vessels

As at the acoustics exhibit, the physical positioning of your disc—that is, your openness to hear and receive the other person's message—is critical for effectiveness in communication. Your body language and that of the person you are talking to is also fundamental to the imparting process. Your bearing and design and that of your companions, subliminally transfers much information. Think again about your vessel and those of your travelling companions. What is their bearing saying on a more subtle level? Below are a few suggested attributes for you to consider:

- open
- closed
- aggressive
- friendly
- questioning
- critical
- nurturing
- relaxed
- bored
- interested
- superior
- guarded
- pensive
- disapproving
- sexual

Body Language

In Chapter 6, we talked about how the body's automatic response to stress is either fight or flight. If the reptilian part of the brain chooses to fight, the back arches and the chest is pushed forward. In instances of flight, the body withdraws as if from an electric shock and becomes smaller or even completely immobilised. Often in interpersonal exchanges, although there is no clear movement, the body postures mirror those used for fight, flight or freeze. These postures give subconscious messages to all parties involved.

8.3 Activity: Interpreting Different Types of Body Language

Skim through a magazine to find some photos or sketches of people and consider the following:

- Are you looking at fight or flee postures?
- How is the person in the picture feeling?
- What can you say about their values?
- What do you think of their energy level?
- How motivated do they look?

- How do they make you feel in response?
- Are there any positive or negative emotions that you are experiencing as a result?
- What are the elements that could inhibit imparting with this person?

For example, a man sitting hunched with his arms folded suggests that perhaps he is angry or depressed. He appears to have withdrawn from the world and remains closed.

What do the positions mean to you? Does it make sense within the larger paradigm of energy flows? Write your responses to the questions above in your journal.

Think about your body language and the clothes you wear. Do they reflect the message that you want to send, or are you sending a double message that is confusing and frustrating to your companions? To be clear and precise about the content of your message, formulate an accurate picture in your mind's eye as a starting point.

8.4 Activity: Reflection

Imagine for a moment being in the shoes of one of your travelling companions. In your journal, reflect what it might be like to live that person's life and share his or her joys and hardships. How do these experiences contribute to who he or she is as a person?

Attitude and Expectation

Your attitude and that of the other person are important in determining the success of any exchange. Expectation is also a very powerful force and is often a determinant of how things turn out. It is as if the environment and those in it sense your expectation, either positive or negative, and apply themselves to fulfil your need—even if it may be detrimental to you as a person.

People with a positive disposition and expectations tend to see negative events as occasional and view them in isolation. When they recall those experiences, they focus solely on the specific person or event. On the other hand, pessimistic people see a negative event as the norm and apply it universally, limiting a positive experience only to a particular event or person. They see a positive as an exception rather than as the rule.

When things go awry, positive people are affected for a shorter period of time before they bounce back to re-evaluate the situation and take action. Negative people act helpless and remain immobilised for longer before pulling themselves together and facing the challenge.

Intimacy or Recognising a Person

Intimacy is the mutual acknowledgement of all parties that they are seen and heard in a caring and unconditional way. This step is sometimes referred to as *recognising* the person. This recognition is achieved by using "I" statements and reflecting what you see and understand of yourself and the other person in an honest, accepting, and loving way.

People who feel honestly and lovingly accepted for who they are will find the courage to reduce their façade and impart in a rich and pure manner. For example, to the man I interpreted as feeling withdrawn and depressed in Activity 8.3, you might say, "Hi, how are you? It looks like you're feeling tired and worried today." He may then tell you that he has lost his job. To reflect your understanding of this, you could respond by saying, "You have lost your job and you are worried about supporting your family …"

8.5 Activity: Recognising the Other Person: Ship Ahoy

Have another look at the pictures from the magazine (Activity 8.3) and think of unthreatening and accepting "I" statements you could use to convey to those people that you have recognised them. The privilege of intimacy is a rare and precious experience. It does however take time, effort and commitment as becomes evident in this simple exercise.

8.6 Activity: Eye Contact

Find a travelling companion with whom you feel comfortable and ask him or her to participate in this exercise with you. It should take about thirty minutes. Find a relaxed and private space and face each other at a distance of about one metre. Set a stopwatch for one minute and look into each other's eyes for that period of time. Say nothing. Focus solely and simply on seeing the other person and allowing the other person to see you.

- What did you notice?
- How did it feel?
- Could you receive and give information at the same time?
- What did you understand from the other person?
- Ask the person if he or she felt accepted and recognized.
- Ask them how he or she found the experience.

Try the exercise a number of times. In time, you will become more relaxed and start to find more subtle elements to the whole experience. Record your findings in your journal.

Ship Ahoy!

Imparting is an ongoing process. As demonstrated at the sound exhibit, the quality of the imparting, no matter how good at the outset, can be marred by outside interference, either deliberate or accidental. So how do we limit this? First, anticipate and plan for potential interference and compensate for it. Below is a list of characteristics that make for the smooth imparting of information.

- *Repetition:* Sending the same message over and over again, as is being done in this content, enables you to fine-tune your inductive and deductive reasoning skills and your appreciation for the need of a gap in time in order to process the world around you from different perspectives.
- *Variety:* Use different mediums either simultaneously or sequentially.
- *Sufficient time:* Time is essential for every successful step in the imparting process. No matter how good the quality of your message—how well-rehearsed, positioned and fine-tuned—it is unlikely to reach the man travelling in his speedboat with a bevy of beauties.
- *Mutual interest:* The other party must be interested and motivated to hear what you have to say. You probably won't have much luck with someone in a balsa-wood raft drifting quietly but aimlessly out to sea. So don't take it personally!
- *Tailored messages:* Make your message specific to your audience, otherwise it will get lost or misinterpreted. A generic message can cause confusion and is a potential seed for conflict between the parties involved—and even for other unsuspecting vessels in close proximity.
- *Appropriateness:* Use examples and language appropriate to your target audience.
- *"I" statements:* Take ownership of your emotions. They are truly and totally yours only, as is your interpretation and perception of any situation.
- *Acceptance of difference:* Recognise, acknowledge and respect the differences that make us unique. To accept that we are all unique and entitled to different viewpoints takes concentrated effort and self-discipline. Consider your travelling companions' vessel designs. Often the simple realisation of their differing focuses in life is sufficient to release you of unrealistic and inappropriate expectations.
- *Respect:* Be respectful of the other party's viewpoint. Respect is an important foundation to imparting.

It is when we act like battleships, judging others in our tone and speech, that we quickly hook their emotions and increase the chances of their responses being equally judgmental and antagonistic. The predictable outcome is war. Alternatively, they may become defensive and withdrawn like a submarine, difficult to detect and converse with.

Craig Ballantyne

8.7 Activity: Hindering and Enhancing Effective Communication

Circle which of the following affects your communication, either facilitating it or impeding it. Reflect in your journal on any insights you have from doing this exercise.

- personal low level of self-attunement
- the low level of self-attunement of the other person
- lack of interest and passive listening
- inarticulateness
- preoccupation and mind-wandering
- emotional block, resistance, and past experiences
- hostility and stereotyping
- charisma and status
- hidden agendas and difficult relationships
- physical environment
- emotions—anger, dislike, prejudice, defensiveness
- assuming what the person is going to say in advance
- prejudging and criticising the response
- pretending to be attentive
- diagnosing and devaluing
- topping the person's content
- permitting the speaker to be inaudible or incomplete

- poor responses that de value the other person for example ridicule, sarcasm, ordering, directing, preaching, moralising

On the other hand, there are many conditions that facilitate effective communication. Some of these are listed below:

- time, trust and an ideal situation
- ability to identify the important themes
- leaving the ownership of the problem in its correct place
- positive self-attunement
- awareness of your feelings and the other person's
- awareness of your value system and the other person's
- respect for the other person and a mutual desire to listen and have a purpose
- listening actively to the physical, emotional, and intellectual content
- understanding at a deeper level why the person is saying what he or she is saying
- clarity of expression—having a clear picture of what you want to say before you say it
- emotions—admit emotions, own them, investigate them, report them, integrate the emotions with the intellect, and positively cope with them
- expressing personal perspective and emotional content with "I" messages
- describing behaviour rather than personality
- self-disclosure—being open, expressing information and emotions
- suspending judgment
- pausing before responding
- empathy—putting yourself in the other person's shoes
- resisting distractions and focusing wholly on the speaker
- reflecting—paraphrasing what has already been said and considering economy of words
- postponing response, pausing to consider before replying
- hindsight analysis

Good communication is a skill—it needs constant practice and refining.

The Signalling Model

There are dynamic elements involved in the imparting process. I have framed them within the theme we have developed so far. The process, though presented in a linear fashion, is in reality dynamic and requires vigilance to ensure all elements remain focused. Therefore:

- Know yourself—be in tune with who you are.
- Move to a neutral spot, perhaps a raft away from your vessel, where you can be objective.
- See yourself.
- See the other party.
- Recognise yourself and the other party using "I" statements.
- Encourage the captain of the other vessels to join you in this neutral and rational place.
- Help the captain to view both your vessels objectively and in an accepting way.
- Loan your telescope if necessary.
- Build a common picture—a shared complete picture reflects true intimacy.
- Acknowledge and respect differences.
- Continuously view and monitor the positioning and feelings of all parties.
- Detect early signs of emotional flooding and take appropriate preventative action.

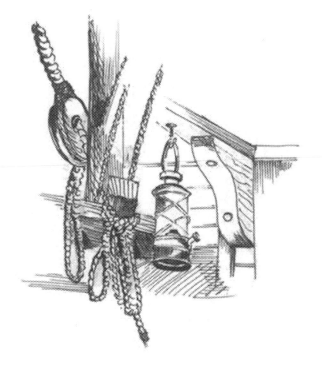

Craig Ballantyne

Summary of the Process of Communication

- Establish the reason for the conversation and the desired result. Often, the reason for the interchange is simply to pass the time in an amicable way. So be it! But by applying integrity, you raise the quality and meaningfulness of the interaction and contribute to a solid foundation for the future. There may be a need to take the relationship deeper when there is indeed a common purpose to pursue.

- See yourself and the other person accurately and without judgment. Identify what the values and motivational elements are from both points of view. Recognise and acknowledge both perspectives using "I" statements.
- Rational discussion of the different points of view and factors under consideration is essential. When your differing perspectives have been recognised and validated, use the helm to steer you both rationally toward the desired outcome.
- Monitor physiological response and emotions. Whenever emotions come to the fore, pause and revisit, seeing and recognising all viewpoints before continuing the discussion. Listen to the subtler elements of the encounter.
- Aim for an amicable conclusion whilst maintaining respect for all viewpoints.

On occasion, we meet less genuine souls who are deliberately determined to undermine and challenge our chosen course, as is the case when we encounter pirates.

CHAPTER 9
Encountering Pirates

No enterprise is more likely to succeed than one concealed from the enemy until it is ripe for execution.

—Niccolo Machiavelli

Craig Ballantyne

Itinerary

In this chapter, you will explore and develop a deeper understanding of how you communicate, resolve conflict, and maintain your boundaries in challenging situations while remaining grounded.

Viewpoints

You will focus on:
- conflict resolution
- assertiveness—setting personal boundaries

Travel bag

You will need:
- your journal
- a ball of string

Introduction

Up until now, we have made the assumption that your conversations have been with other travellers and captains whose vessels may have been of a very different design and purpose but in essence were of good intent. This is not always the case—sometimes, you encounter pirates! These are crafts that have no intention of "seeing" or "hearing" you; they're only determined to commandeer your ship and ransack your treasure. We will now explore your natural style in managing conflict and how to maintain your boundaries in a mature and contained manner.

Transactional Analysis (TA) Communication Model

On our journey so far, the concepts presented were in terms of characteristics reflected in your sailing craft, the Aurora model. However, several of the key concepts mentioned have their foundation in the transactional analysis communication model developed by Dr. Eric Berne in the 1950s (Harris 1967). Originally trained in psychoanalysis, Berne wanted a theory that could be understood and available to everyone. Berne stated that we have three parts of ourselves: the Parent (values and beliefs), the Adult (rational thinking), and the Child (emotions).

The Parent

The Parent reflects our values and beliefs. These facets of ourselves are laid down in the first five years of our lives and are generally absorbed from our caregivers—thus the use of the term *parent*. If we have simply absorbed and not processed the values of our caregivers and hold them to be true for all people, we have an ethnocentric view of the world. It is only through exploring other cultures and realities—and using our Adult—that we challenge these absorbed values and develop our own values and beliefs and identity. This usually happens during adolescence, when we consciously separate ourselves from our parents and family to explore the world of our peers and other cultures. We then choose what we would like to hold as important in our lives and what we would like to shed from our caregivers' view of the world. The Adult enables this process.

Berne talks about the Parent as having a number of different positive and negative dimensions. A Positive Parent would be caring, honest, loyal, hard-working and have high morals. The role of the Negative Parent is to set boundaries and maintain a sense of order. This is achieved through judging, being critical, controlling, and making decisions. Without the Negative Parent, we would live in chaos. There is also the potential for the Parent to be manipulative and damaging, and I have labelled this as a Double Negative Parent. For those of you that have done some maths, in this instance this does not equal a positive!

The Adult

The Adult refers to the scientist within us. It is how we explore the world, by asking those Socratic questions of what, who, why, how, when, and where. It is through the Adult that we challenge reality and ask ourselves why we are the way we are and what we want to change. This book has all been about developing the Adult part of you. It is with a well-developed Adult that we are consciously able to change our habitual patterns of behaviour and thinking.

The Child

The Child refers to our emotions: these tend to have become a part of who we are prior to any developed sense of language. As a consequence, it is not always easy for us to identify and access our emotions. The Child also presents in a number of dimensions. The Positive Child is trusting, energetic, enthusiastic, adventurous, joyous, creative, and innocent. The Negative Child can either be overt in presentation—angry, loud or aggressive, or covert—withdrawn, sulky, anxious and depressed.

The concepts of TA are incorporated in the Aurora model, with the hull and keel (Parent), the helm (Adult), and the rudder (Child). Examples of these characteristics are laid out in the following diagram.

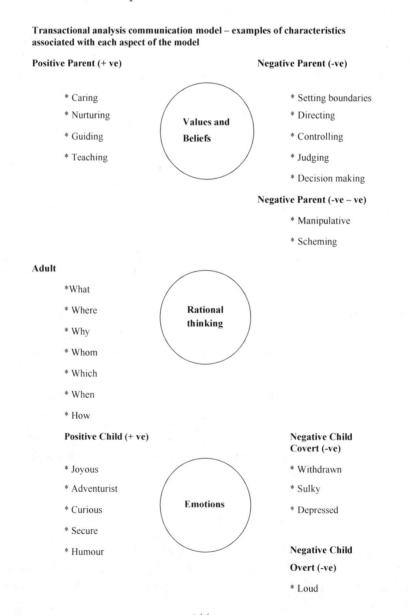

Transactional analysis communication model – examples of characteristics associated with each aspect of the model

Positive Parent (+ ve)

* Caring
* Nurturing
* Guiding
* Teaching

Values and Beliefs

Negative Parent (-ve)

* Setting boundaries
* Directing
* Controlling
* Judging
* Decision making

Negative Parent (-ve – ve)

* Manipulative
* Scheming

Adult

*What
* Where
* Why
* Whom
* Which
* When
* How

Rational thinking

Positive Child (+ ve)

* Joyous
* Adventurist
* Curious
* Secure
* Humour

Emotions

Negative Child Covert (-ve)

* Withdrawn
* Sulky
* Depressed

Negative Child Overt (-ve)

* Loud

Constructive Communication Transactions

Constructive communication occurs when we affirm and reflect mutually affirming values, beliefs, intensions and emotions. This connection can occur in a number of different ways as is explained below.

Positive Parent to Positive Parent: When we engage with another person, we engage with their Parent, Adult or Child. In the engagement, if we discover that our Parent dimensions are similar, then we will feel comfortable and connected. For example, if we have the same political, religious or child-rearing views, we will happily discuss these at length.

Positive Parent to Positive Parent

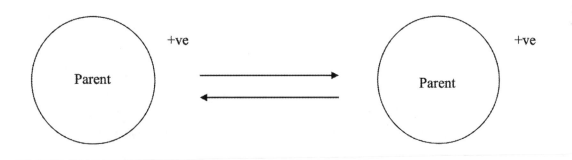

Negative Parent to Negative Parent: This combination is viewed as constructive when both parties are in agreement. For example, when two people are discussing their concerns about binge drinking, stating that it is unhealthy and dangerous for children under the drinking age, they may seem critical and judgmental. However, if both parties have the same values and beliefs and agree on this issue, they are comfortable with each other's judgments and critical comments.

Negative Parent to Negative Parent

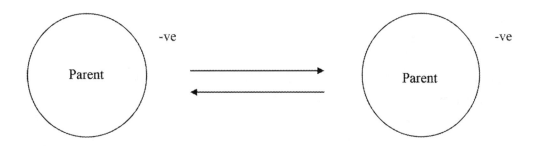

Adult to Adult: In an Adult-to-Adult connection, we are sharing information and feel unthreatened and comfortable together—for example, if we were engaged in a fact-finding mission or processing information for a work project.

Adult to Adult

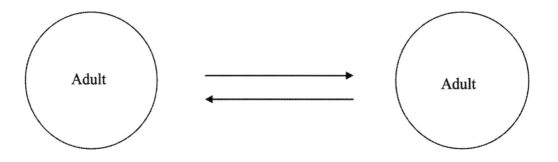

Positive Child to Positive Child: Similarly, we can have a Positive Child to Positive Child experience, sharing fun and laughter and a sense of joy in the world. When we are both having fun and exploring together and laughing, there will be little tension between us.

Positive Child to Positive Child

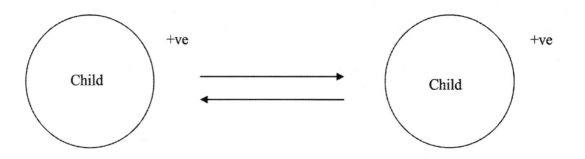

Obviously, this is not the case in a Negative Child to Negative Child experience, which is felt to be destructive by both parties.

Positive Parent to Positive Child: Alternatively, the other person could be guiding or teaching us, in essence treating us like a child using their Positive Parent. They would be engaging our Positive Child, giving us a feeling of being secure, nurtured and cared for.

Positive Parent to Positive Child

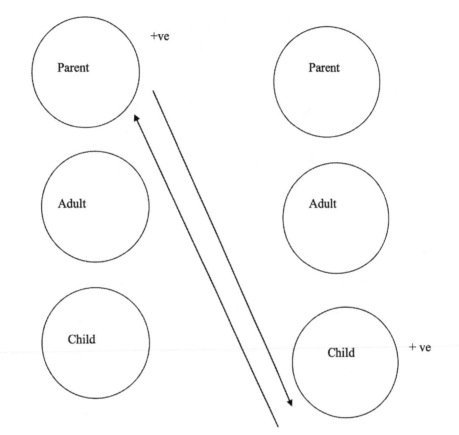

Destructive Transactions

Destructive transactions occur when we do not share the same values and beliefs or when the other person has an agenda of his or her own—or, as mentioned previously, when we engage our Negative Child with the other person's Negative Child.

Negative Parent to Withdrawn Covert Negative Child: This situation can occur when we are with someone whose Negative Parent is contrary to ours—that is, we have different values and beliefs, perhaps on politics, religion, or ethnic point-of-view—or if we are with a person with a Double Negative Parent—that is, someone who is trying to manipulate and control us. We may choose not to challenge them but rather to withdraw. In this case, we can instinctively revert to our Covert Negative Child, becoming withdrawn, sulky or depressed. The person with the

Covert Child response to conflict may experience damage to his or her self-esteem and sense of self-worth over time. If this pattern is not constructively addressed, it can lead to depression for the person demonstrating Covert Negative Child behaviour.

Negative Parent to Withdrawn Covert Negative Child

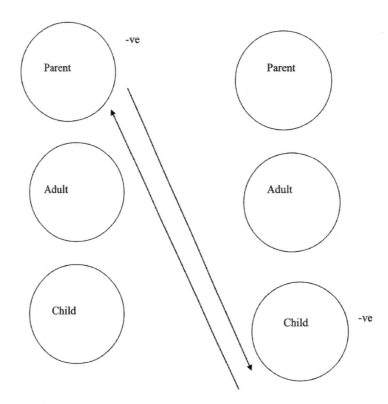

Negative Child to Negative Child: If we engage our Negative Child—either overtly, by being aggressive and angry, or covertly, by being withdrawn, sulky and depressed—this is another destructive form of engagement, leaving both parties with unresolved issues and emotional damage.

Negative Child to Negative Child

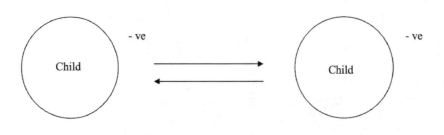

It is important to note that the Adult in both parties is missing in all of these exchanges. It is only when we engage the Adult that we are able to resolve conflict constructively.

Negative Parent to Outward Overt Negative Child: The other person's Negative Parent may trigger our Overt Negative Child, whereby we become angry. This, in turn, can trigger our own Negative Parent or Double Negative Parent, so that we become attacking and condescending toward the other person. This pattern inevitably triggers the other person's Overt Negative Child to become defensive and attacking, setting up a perpetuating destructive cycle.

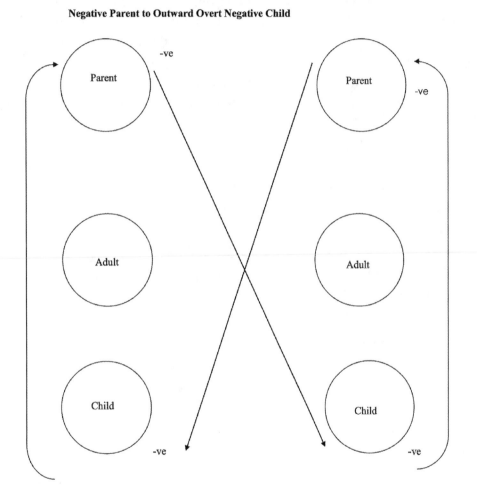

Negative Parent to Outward Overt Negative Child

Please note the absence of the Adult; the Adult is our rational self, the part that asks why, what, how, when, and where, and this is necessary to understand the situation fully and to develop potential solutions that could resolve the conflict.

Stages of Constructively Managing Conflict

Managing conflict constructively requires the incorporation of all of the constructive communications previously mentioned in a dance that brings us to a place of rational, emotionally controlled discussion, whereby we are able to achieve and negotiate some form of resolution or simply agree to disagree.

1. Recognize your own emotions and your somatic (physical) response and bring these under control by taking a deep breath, counting to ten, or going for a long walk until you feel contained and grounded and able to calmly engage with the other person.

2. Recognize commonly held values and beliefs that the other person holds and which are reflective of your own. It is important that you are authentic in this, as you will otherwise be seen to be a Double Negative Parent—that is, someone who is manipulative and controlling. Reflect to the other person that you recognize his or her values and beliefs and acknowledge that the individual holds them to be important. By doing so, the other person will feel recognized and heard and will feel less vulnerable, and therefore more open to hearing a different point of view.

3. If appropriate, reflect that you also understand the emotions that are attached to the other person's beliefs and/or the circumstances of the situation.

4. Reflect and articulate your own values and beliefs that are in common with the other person.

5. Engage the other person's Adult by asking what he or she thinks the issues are and how they could be resolved.

6. Share your own thoughts on the issue.

Stages of Constructively Managing Conflict

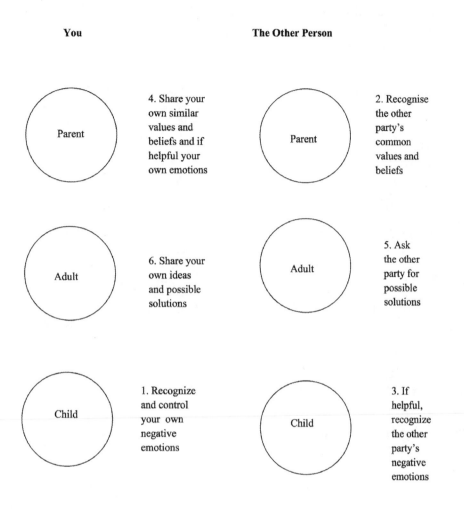

You   The Other Person

Parent — 4. Share your own similar values and beliefs and if helpful your own emotions

Parent — 2. Recognise the other party's common values and beliefs

Adult — 6. Share your own ideas and possible solutions

Adult — 5. Ask the other party for possible solutions

Child — 1. Recognize and control your own negative emotions

Child — 3. If helpful, recognize the other party's negative emotions

9.1 Activity: Explore the Model from Your Own Experience

Using the template on the following page, analyse a number of transactions that have been both constructive and destructive. Once you feel you have an understanding of the elements of the TA communication model, reflect on a conflict that has occurred and how you have managed it. With your new insights from this model, reflect on whether and how you would manage it differently. Record your insights in your journal.

Transactional Analysis Communication Model

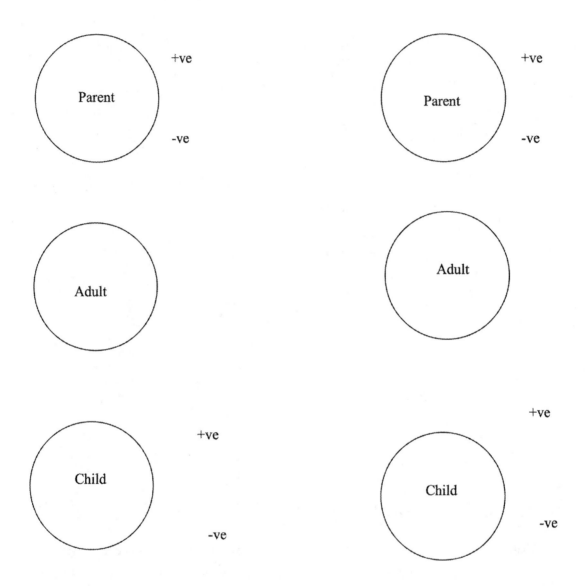

Battle Tactics: Positively Managing Conflict

Our ways of managing conflict are habitual and have been with us since we were babies. In the following exercise, explore your natural style in resolving conflict.

9.2 Activity: Explore Your Natural Conflict-Resolution Style

Complete the "Passive Accepting/Assertive/Directive Controlling Conflict Questionnaire," which will give an indication of your natural conflict-resolution style. You may have to focus on a specific situation or person, as your style often changes depending on the circumstances and the people you are with.

Passive Accepting/Assertive/Directive Controlling Conflict Questionnaire

Adapted from the Thomas–Kilmann Conflict Mode Instrument (Thomas 2002)

Consider situations in which you find your wishes differing from those of another person. How do you usually respond to such situations? Below there are groupings of three statements describing possible behavioral responses. For each item, please circle the A, B or C statement, whichever is most characteristic of your own behaviour. In many cases, none of the choices will be very typical of your behaviour, but please select the response that you would be more likely to use.

Question 1
  A. I make some effort to get my way.
  B. I attempt to get all concerned and issues immediately out in the open.
  C. There are times when I let others take responsibility for solving the problem.

Question 2
  A. Rather than negotiate the things on which we disagree, I try to stress those things upon which we both agree.
  B. I sometimes sacrifice my own wishes for the wishes of the other person.
  C. I try to win my position.

Question 3
  A. I sometimes avoid taking positions that would create controversy.
  B. I press to get my point made.
  C. I am usually firm in pursuing my goals.

Question 4
  A. I attempt to get all concerns and issues immediately out in the open.
  B. I try to convince the other person of the merits of my position.
  C. I try to do what is necessary to avoid tensions.

Question 5
  A. I like to be in charge.
  B. I might try to soothe the other person's feelings and preserve our relationship.

    C. I tell my ideas and ask other people for theirs.

Question 6
    A. I try to avoid creating unpleasantness for myself.
    B. I try to find a compromise solution.
    C. I try to show the other person the logic and benefits of my position.

Question 7
    A. I attempt to deal with all of the other person's concerns.
    B. I assert my wishes.
    C. I might try to soothe the other person's feelings and preserve our relationship.

Question 8
    A. I try not to hurt the other person's feelings.
    B. I always share the problem with the other person so that we can work it out.
    C. I like to take control of the situation.

Question 9
    A. I try to convince the other person of the merits of my position.
    B. I try to postpone the issue until I have had some time to think it over.
    C. In approaching negotiations, I try to be considerate of the other person's wishes.

Question 10
    A. If it makes the other person happy, I might let him maintain his views.
    B. I always lean toward a direct discussion of the problem.
    C. I prefer to have things my own way.

On the table below, circle your responses in the appropriate column and then total the number of responses in each column. This will give an indication of your natural style of behaviour.

	Passive / accepting	Assertive	Directive/ controlling
1.	C	B	A
2.	B	A	C
3.	A	C	B
4.	C	A	B
5.	B	C	A
6.	A	B	C

	Passive / accepting	Assertive	Directive/ controlling
7.	C	A	B
8.	A	B	C
9.	B	C	A
10.	A	B	C
	Total: _____	Total: _____	Total: _____

How did you fare?

Internal (Intrinsic) and External (Extrinsic) Motivation

Individuals with an internal or intrinsic motivation engage in and complete a task for the real pleasure of the task itself—for example, the joy of playing a piece of music flawlessly and with melody simply for the pure pleasure of it. Externally or extrinsically motivated people engage in an activity for the benefit of the external rewards—such as recognition by others, status, money, and power.

In terms of the model presented, it is suggested that submissive/passive people may be either intrinsically motivated or completely content with their role and station in life, in that they are living and doing what they feel is of value, and that is reward in and of itself. Or they may be extrinsically motivated and want recognition from others. If this is not achieved or given, they can then feel unappreciated and burnt out. In managing conflict, submissive/passive people tend to be prepared to lose so that others win and/or feel comfortable, in order to keep the peace.

Externally motivated submissive/passive people tend to give until they are completely exhausted, at which stage they can either move to a place of depression and withdrawal (Covert Angry Negative Child) or become loud, aggressive, directive and controlling (Overt Negative Child). However, this is not their natural style, and they then revert to submissive and passive behaviour, often feeling guilty and sorry for their outburst.

Power people tend to be externally motivated and approach conflict in a controlling and directive manner, with the intention of winning while the other person loses. They need to win so that they can maintain their position. If they are not in control and lose, they tend to feel insecure and/or angry.

Assertive people, on the other hand, tend to be internally motivated and approach conflict with a win-win attitude, putting their needs and the needs of others on the table so as to reach a workable solution for everyone involved. Whatever the outcome, they are at peace within themselves.

Assertive people tend to follow the TA communication model outlined previously, recognizing other people and their needs as well as their own needs. They remain rational in their search for a solution that meets the needs of everyone involved. Usually, they are able to maintain their boundaries.

Submissive/Passive	Assertive	Controlling/Directing
Lose–Win Tend to lose, allowing others to win Motivation: Intrinsic or Extrinsic	Win–Win Tend to look for a win–win outcome Motivation: Intrinsic	Win–Lose Tend to need to win while others lose so that they can maintain control Motivation: Extrinsic

 9.3 Activity: Reflect on Your Understanding of Different Styles

Now reflect on how each of these specific types of people feel to you and record it on your table. What motivates them? How do you view their behaviours? Use the insights that follow to guide your thoughts, and note them in your journal.

Which behaviours do you associate with submissive/passive people—positive or negative? In some cultures and religions, submissive and passive behaviour is seen as highly superior. It would be viewed as someone having a strong sense of community and respect. In other circumstances, it may be seen as weak and lacking direction or backbone.

Similarly, directive and controlling people can be seen both positively and negatively. They play a definite role in getting things done and generating outcomes, but this can be negative if they are seen as a Double Negative Parent, manipulative and controlling. What behaviours are typical of directive and controlling people, positive or negative? What behaviours are typical of assertive people?

Submissive people can be intrinsically or extrinsically motivated. If intrinsically motivated, they are often at peace and very content within themselves. However, if they are submissive in the hope of feeling valued and connected with an individual or the community where they live, they may feel frustrated, depressed and unappreciated.

Assertive people, on the other hand, tend to be internally motivated and because of their tendency to be collective in their approach, they seek the best outcome for everyone involved. They generally feel good about themselves and not vulnerable. Their intrinsic motivation is self-determining and does not rely on reinforcement from outsiders.

Directing people may feel a sense of status and power. They may feel successful and superior and tend to be externally motivated in their actions. However, if they are not successful and in control, they may feel insecure, angry and vulnerable.

An example of the characteristics associated with each is given below.

Submissive Passive	Assertive	Controlling/Directing
Behaviours Positive: Caring, nurturing, serving, accommodating Negative: Self-sacrificing, not putting their point of view across	*Behaviours* Positive: Good listeners, inclusive, put their own point of view across, open to other points of view, open to negotiate for a win–win solution, prepared to make unpopular decisions that they believe to be correct, maintain personal boundaries	*Behaviours* Positive: Get the job done, task-orientated, take control, clear in what they set out to achieve Negative: Loud, do not take others points of view into account, can be manipulative, aggressive, and dishonest
Feelings Positive: Feel connected, humble, and at peace with themselves and the world. Negative: Feel unappreciated, used, and not respected; feelings of fear, rejection, being unheard, vulnerability, exhaustion Angry (Overt Negative Child), Depressed (Covert Negative Child)	*Feelings* Positive: Feel in control, like and respect themselves, do not take others reactions to themselves personally. Secure, confident, open (Positive Child)	*Feelings* Positive: Powerful, strong, in control, superior (Positive Child) Negative: When not in control, secure, fearful and anxious (Negative Child)

☙ 9.4 Activity: Complete the Conflict-Resolution Table

What is your motivation and conflict resolution style? Give examples of behaviours and feelings that are typical of you. How does it support you in maintaining your boundaries and in resolving conflict with significant people in your life?

What dynamic would you like to change and how do you think you could do that? Make a note in your journal of your insights and any changes that you are planning to make with respect to how you manage conflict in the future. Reflect any insights you have in your journal.

Submissive/Passive	Assertive	Controlling/Directing
Lose–Win Motivation: Intrinsic/Extrinsic	Win–Win Motivation: Intrinsic	Win–Lose Motivation: Extrinsic
Behaviours Positive: Negative:	*Behaviours* Positive: Negative:	*Behaviours* Positive: Negative:
Feelings Positive: Negative:	*Feelings* Positive: Negative:	*Feelings* Positive: Negative

Your Personal Territory: Assertively Developing Your Personal Boundaries

Our lives are filled with boundaries. Some are immutable, like those of continents— mountains, rivers and seas; some are political; others are conceptual, for example, race, culture and economic disposition; and some are territorial, like your neighbourhood, garden wall or front door. Finally, there is our personal boundary, the sense of personal space around us. All boundaries have a functional impact on energy flow and, depending on whether they are present or perceived, they impact our being, thoughts, emotions, and physical and behavioural responses. In the next exercise, we are going to explore your personal-space boundaries.

Personal boundaries are the invisible physical, emotional and mental limits we use to demarcate our personal space. Boundaries vary in terms of their flexibility and permeability. They are important in maintaining a clear sense of self by separating how we think and feel from the thoughts and feelings of others. They also protect us from others by helping us to decide to whom we want to be close. This keeps us from being manipulated or violated. Finally, they help filter and make sense of information from our environment.

Healthy boundaries allow a balance between self-disclosure to significant others and privacy. They give the individual the freedom to choose when, to whom, and how much they disclose. Individuals with healthy boundaries have a strong sense of identity and self-worth and expect reciprocity in relationships. When individuals have healthy boundaries, they are able to say yes or no without guilt, anger or fear. They do not tolerate abuse or disrespect, or take on other people's problems.

Individuals with unhealthy boundaries, on the other hand, tend to be inflexible and have difficulty developing intimate relationships with others. They have a fear of being hurt or taken advantage of. They also struggle with and have difficulty identifying their wants, needs, and feelings. They fear abandonment or suffocation, and they avoid close relationships. As a consequence of weak boundaries, they tend to say yes to all requests because of their fear of rejection and abandonment. They tend to tolerate abuse or disrespectful treatment and may even feel that they deserve to be treated poorly. They generally avoid conflict, focusing on pleasing those around them. They also tend to take on the feelings of others.

Strategies for Developing Healthy Boundaries

You can develop healthy boundaries by becoming conscious and self-aware, by defining your sense of self, and by understanding your feelings, thoughts, beliefs, values, attitudes, and needs. It involves defining behaviours you find unacceptable, learning to trust your own responses, and finally developing your communication and being able to say no.

9.5 Activity: Exploring Your Personal Boundaries

Reconsider all the exercises you have done so far and again reflect in your journal on where you maintain your boundaries and where you don't, and what changes you would like to make in your future interactions with specific individuals.

9.6 Activity: Exploring the Dynamics of Your Personal Field

Take a length of wool or string approximately five metres long. Find a spot in a room where you feel comfortable and have a reasonable amount of space around you. Now arrange the yarn on the floor fully around you so that the ends reconnect. It can be any shape that you like. Stand within the shape and note how you feel. Take your time with this exercise—what you are learning to experience is real and very subtle. When you are fully in touch with how you feel, draw the shape and dimensions in your journal and make a note of your feelings.

Now I would like you to imagine that you are in a crowded market somewhere in the heat of North Africa. People are all around you. Children are pulling at your clothes and asking for sweets. You can only partly understand what people are saying. When you have fully imagined the scene, place the yarn around you again, ensuring that it forms a continuous line. What is the shape now and how does it make you feel? What is the difference in shape and size between this boundary and the original one you placed about yourself? Note the difference in your journal.

Now place a perfect circle around you. Stand in the middle. Close your eyes and imagine yourself being firmly rooted into the ground, roots spreading out from your feet deep and wide to ensure that you are stable and firmly connected to the earth. Experience again the effect of simply changing the yarn boundary around you.

It is important to note that this is something you can achieve consciously at any time, without the assistance of the yarn. The shape and expanse of your personal field can be consciously monitored and manoeuvered. Consider mentally centring and feeling it around you. Think of the times when you spread yourself too thin or feel fragmented. At times like these, your personal field may have been expanded to include too many people and activities. When you feel like this, deliberately think about re-centring yourself. Consciously bring your personal field in to a comfortable close protective cloak around you with your feet firmly rooted to the earth. Ensure that your field is large enough to encircle you completely, particularly the region of space behind you.

Monitor your breathing and listen to your body. Note which parts are tense. Check how your heart is beating and take the time to allow the rate to return to normal. Concentrate on relaxing all your muscles. Regain your sense of posture and control. In moments of crisis or confrontation, ensure that the imaginary boundary behind you is sufficient to give you a sense of security.

This can be a useful exercise when you consciously want to take a position and maintain your boundaries, particularly in an adversarial situation.

Manning the Helm When Our Boundaries Are Challenged

When our boundaries are challenged, we naturally withdraw and in time may become depressed and/or angry. Anger is a natural emotion that we start to experience within the first four months of life. It is usually a response to a demand or an expectation that is not met. Physiologically, when angry, the body gears up for action, with an increase in the heart and breathing rates, blood pressure, and muscle tightness.

When we become overtaken by anger, the emotions associated with the event flood the amygdala and immobilize rational thinking. The body fills with tension, anticipating a fight-flight or -freeze response. Because your amygdala is saturated, you will not engage in rational thinking, which occurs in the frontal cortex of the brain. It is like a ship firing all its cannons at once. It causes great havoc with the stability of the ship, risks all hands on deck being injured in the chaos and is potentially lethal to other vessels forming part of the same fleet. In the frenzy of activity, there is slim chance of actually hitting the targeted enemy.

In the following exercise, I would like you to consider a relatively recent situation in which you were angry. Regrettably, I am going to have to ask you to imagine and relive the situation in your mind. This will evoke many of the same negative emotions and bodily responses that you originally experienced, but hopefully the learning that you gain from this exercise will justify reliving this situation.

It will also illustrate to you how your negative thoughts can have a negative affect and how vulnerable you are to your thoughts mentally, physically and emotionally. Your thoughts are registered and recorded physiologically. The fact that your body can react physiologically when recording a memory clearly demonstrates this. This is why the genuine act of forgiveness is so freeing for both parties. It allows for release of this tension.

When dealing with anger, if you constantly monitor your feelings and tensions and allow them to dissipate, tension is not stored. If stored, tension negatively affects your health and has the potential to block and sabotage your emotions in future encounters. Staying present and allowing tension to dissipate immediately is the healthiest approach to managing your anger and conflict experiences.

9.7 Activity: Recalling a Situation That Caused You to Feel Angry

Think about a fairly recent situation when you were feeling extremely angry. Imagine the event as vividly as possible and then answer the following questions in your journal.

- What was the situation? Describe it in detail.
- What was the time of day, month and season?
- What did you think about the situation?
- How did you feel about the situation?
- What was the setting?
- What did you think about the setting?
- How did you feel about the setting?
- Who was present?
- What do you think about these people?
- How did you feel about these people?
- Why were they there?

- What was the conflict about?
- How did they behave?
- What do you think they were thinking?
- What do you think they were feeling?
- What were their beliefs in relation to the issue?
- What were their feelings in relation to the issue?
- How did they express their emotions?
- What values and beliefs were crossed in the conflict?
- What expectations were not met?
- Were these expectations reasonable?
- What were your thoughts at the time?
- Is there a typical pattern of behaviour for you and the parties involved that is reflected in this conflict?
- Can you understand the other parties' points of view, their perspectives?
- Can you empathise with them?
- Is there a solution that could accommodate all points of view?
- How could it work?
- How would that make you feel?
- How would it make the other parties feel?
- Do you blame the other parties?
- Do you take any responsibility yourself?
- How can you prevent this from happening again in the future?
- How do you feel now?
- What were the insights that you gained from this exercise?

Assess the Situation

- Are there any extraneous variables that could be contributing to my feelings? For example, am I hungry?
- What is the issue at stake?
- What are the underlying, subconscious issues that are not being mentioned but which have contributed to the situation? Who or what is responsible?
- What are my views and values? How can I express these in a non-threatening manner?
- What are my physiological responses? (Pause long enough for the heart rate to return to normal.)
- What is my body language? Is it relaxed or is it threatening? (If you are feeling tension in your muscles, pause and consciously wait for the tension to dissipate. Remain in control of your bodily functions. Acknowledge that you are feeling threatened. Consciously respond to your body's alarm signals.)

- What are the demands and expectations of all parties involved? What do we have in common? If we stand shoulder-to-shoulder, can we see each other's perspectives?
- What are the other parties' views and values? How can I reflect that I understand their points of view? Acknowledge their viewpoints?
- How can I acknowledge their feelings and emotions?

Do a grounding exercise or relaxation technique and release all the physical tensions and emotions that revisiting this experience may have created. Listen to your heartbeat. Breathe deeply and wait for your heartbeat to return to normal.

Negative and Positive Core Beliefs

Often it is our own negative core beliefs that trigger our emotional response. On the list below, consider which of the beliefs you associate with yourself and the particular event you have just analysed. How true are the negative beliefs that you have identified? What are the positive beliefs that you would prefer to associate with yourself and the event?

9.8 Activity: Assess Your Beliefs

Take yourself to your safe place. Reflect in your journal any insights you have about the validity of your thoughts, and how they may influence the memory of past and future events.

List of Negative Cognitions	Positive Cognitions

Defectiveness

I'm not good enough.	I am good fine as I am.
I don't deserve to be loved.	I deserve to be loved.
I am a bad person.	I am a good (loving) person.
I am incompetent.	I am competent.
I am inadequate.	I am worthwhile.
I am shameful.	I am honourable.
I am unlovable.	I am lovable.
I deserve only bad things.	I deserve good things.
I am permanently damaged.	I am/can be healthy.
I am ugly	I am lovable.
I do not deserve …	I deserve …
I am stupid/not smart enough.	I am able to learn.
I am insignificant/unimportant.	I am significant/important.
I am a disappointment.	I'm okay just the way I am.
I deserve to die.	I deserve to live.
I deserve to be miserable.	I deserve to be happy.
I am different	I am okay as I am.
I have to be perfect.	I am fine the way I am.

Action

I should have done something.	I did the best I could.
I did something wrong.	I learnt/can learn from it.
I should have known better.	I did the best I could/I can learn.
I am shameful/stupid/a bad person.	I am fine as I am.
I am inadequate/weak.	I am adequate/strong.

Safety/Vulnerability

I cannot trust anyone.	I can choose whom to trust.
I cannot protect myself.	I can learn to protect myself.
I am in danger.	It's over: I am safe now.
I am not safe.	I am safe now.
I'm going to die.	I am safe now.
It's not okay to show my emotions.	I can safely show my emotions.

Power/Control

I am not in control.	I am in control now.
I am powerless.	I now have choices.
I cannot get what I want.	I can get what I want.
I cannot stand up for myself.	I can make my needs known.
I cannot let it out.	I can choose to relate.
I cannot be trusted.	I can be trusted.
I cannot trust myself.	I can learn/to trust myself.
I cannot trust my judgment.	I can trust my judgment.
I am a failure/will fail.	I can succeed.
I cannot succeed.	I can succeed.
I have to please everyone.	I can be myself/make mistakes.
I can't handle it/I'm out of control.	I can handle it.

(Adapted from Shapiro 2008)

During the previous exercises, you should have gained some insight into the views and perspectives of your "opponent." This deeper understanding should help soften your stand and your negative experience, if only marginally. You will need to start to apply this process *before* the amygdala is flooded with emotion and immobilizes your rational-thinking cortex and neocortex. This will require diligent and close monitoring of your feelings, particularly your negative feelings.

Once you have experienced managing your emotions in a testing situation and avoided losing control, it will be easier to repeat that level of control in the future. Express and recognize your behaviour, thoughts, and feelings, using "I" statements. Assertive behaviour requires that you take full responsibility for how you feel. That means not blaming anyone else for your feelings in a given situation. Viktor Frankl has shown us that you can indeed choose your emotions in the harshest of realities, even when facing death in a concentration camp. Admit your beliefs, values, and circumstances, using "I" statements. In expressing anger, you need to be aware of your emotions and their roots.

Recognize the other person using "I" statements reflecting their predicament, values, and how you think that makes them feel. Stay in this stage of recognition until the other person feels heard and the emotional energy has dissipated. Only when this has been achieved can any form of quality long-term resolution be achieved.

What are the things you can do to accommodate all parties involved? Take time to respond. Pause, think, reflect, and relax. Ask yourself if the level of anger you are expressing is appropriate to the situation, or if should you just it let go, valuing your emotional health and balance over the potential gains of the conflict.

Be prepared to forgive and forget. Forgiving is actually an incredibly enriching and empowering experience. Forgiveness often comes with the insight that people often do what they do because they know no better.

The Power of Silence

Never underestimate the power of silence. I once applied this strategy with one of my daughter's schoolteachers. When my daughter was six years old, as far as my values were concerned, her teacher had been extremely cruel and vindictive to her and had seriously damaged her self-confidence and self-esteem. It took more than two years for the damage to be repaired. My anger was so great that I arranged to meet with the teacher and for my husband to be present, as I was seriously concerned that in my fury I might resort to verbal abuse. I was counting on his presence to be a calming influence.

At the last minute, my husband was unable to join us. Fearful of the potential outcome and also fully aware that my daughter would be at this woman's mercy for another six months, I decided I would not say anything. I would simply listen to her side of the story and make another appointment when I knew that my husband could be present.

The outcome was amazing! A very defensive and irate first-grade teacher greeted me. She was smoking a cigarette furiously and pacing the length of the classroom. This lady was so intimidating that few mothers had the courage to challenge her. The headmistress had confided in me that even she was afraid of the woman. I said nothing; I simply monitored my breathing, heart rate, and body language. In time, her ranting and raving gave way and was slowly followed by self-recrimination and a confession. Finally, she acknowledged she had been in the wrong and apologized for what she had done. I had not said a single word!

Positively managing your feelings frees your energy and the sense of control positively impacts your health, your general vital energy, and your self-esteem. In many of the exercises you have completed so far, the purpose has been to prod you to explore who you are and to become more aware and more conscious. Although it is often laborious to examine these elements in fine detail, it is only when this is done and the information is understood within the broader context that a true and deeper understanding is achieved. We don't just drift into a position of deeper understanding, we attain it by making a conscious decision and applying continuous effort to achieve it.

When you next feel overwhelmed by an emotion, ask yourself what underlying root of the emotion is. Is the emotion appropriate to your current situation, or is it reflective of another issue in your life? Perhaps it is something recorded in your subconscious and unrelated to the present situation.

What are the negative thoughts associated with the situation and what alternative positive thoughts could you reframe it with? The more you are in tune with who you are and what your body is telling you, the more quickly you will be able to recognize these potentially marauding vagabonds and outmanoeuvre them. Listen to your intuition: it is your sixth sense. Choose only the battles you know you will win. In cases where you know you will not win, tactfully withdraw and save your resources for another day, when you will be able to draw in reinforcements and be in a better position to confront the assailant.

If confrontation is unavoidable, be Machiavellian in your approach. Take the initiative. Be like the submarine, very aware of your position and resources, unseen, stealthy and unpredictable. When launching your torpedo, do so with intent on a clear target. With awareness, vision and foresight, be as creative as possible in outmanoeuvring the potential hazard prior to your opponent's attack.

This brings us to the next chapter, on creativity—navigating by the stars.

CHAPTER 10
Navigating by the Stars

Famous

The river is famous to the fish.

The loud voice is famous to silence,
which knew it would inherit the earth
before anybody said so.

The cat sleeping on the fence is famous to
the birds
watching him from the birdhouse.

The tear is famous, briefly, to the cheek.

The idea you carry close to your bosom
is famous to your bosom.

The boot is famous to the earth,
more famous than the dress shoe,
which is famous only to floors.

The bent photograph is famous to the one who
carries it
and not at all famous to the one who is pictured.

I want to be famous to shuffling men
who smile while crossing streets,
sticky children in grocery lines,
famous as the one who smiled back.

I want to be famous in the way a pulley is
famous,
or a buttonhole, not because it did anything
spectacular,
but because it never forgot what it could do.

—Naomi Shihab Nye

A discovery is said to be an accident meeting a prepared mind.

—Albert Szent-Gyoygyi

Did you ever observe to whom the accidents happen? Chance favours only the prepared mind.

—Louis Pasteur

One does not discover new lands without consenting to lose sight of the shore for a very long time.

—Andre Gide

Imagination is more important than knowledge.

—Albert Einstein

Itinerary

In this chapter, you will explore and develop personal creativity and innovative characteristics against the backdrop of research of typically inventive people.

Viewpoint

You will focus on:
- creativity

Travel Bag

You will need:
- your journal
- blank paper
- felt-tip pens and coloured crayons

Introduction

Creativity plays an important role in expanding your horizons, your opportunities and your inventiveness so as to maximise your resources. It provides the impetus toward inspiration and is a powerful force in helping you to maximise your resources. Creativity is a function of the positive inner child and it has the added potential to bring joy and a spirit of adventure to your life. We all have the fundamental ability to be more creative in our lives.

In the realm of science, the definitive source of creativity remains uncharted. Its physiological centre is still to be located. Creative people exhibit a variety of characteristics, many of which are opposites. Extensive research by Csikszentmihalyi (1997) reflects that creative people are a synthesis of all potential elements of their personality, actively applied and focused on a particular field of knowledge or domain. Csikszentmihalyi used the term *flow* to express the harnessing of this creative potential. Typically, people who experience flow express deep enjoyment of and total involvement in the important aspects of their lives.

In this chapter, you will be encouraged to unleash your creative inner child by actively seeking to expand your knowledge and provide a platform to follow your intuition and explore the unknown in order to reach your full potential. It is through your persistent questioning and sharing of information that you will tap into the unknown window of the Johari model.

Creative people are compelled to follow an urge or a hunch through to completion. In doing so, they gain a greater understanding of themselves and the universe. They then act on these new ideas and insights and they disseminate this new knowledge to others.

I suspect that, in time, research will find that creativity is an art that uses our whole being, drawing upon every fibre of who we are and linking us with the whole of the universe. The *"Aha!"* we feel when we discover a new insight is an experience that resonates through our whole being. It tingles throughout our bodies. It is as though a bolt of energy has been transmitted from the universe through to our core of understanding.

In this leg of the journey, we will view the characteristics identified by Csikszentmihalyi's research that are common to creative people and those recognised by the wider society as creative through prizes and awards. Through this, and with the help of additional exercises, you will have the opportunity to access and develop your own creativity and reap the benefits and enjoyment of being more imaginative, inventive and resourceful.

Craig Ballantyne

Creativity Explained Using the Sailing-Craft Analogy

Typically, successful creative people are complex personalities with a multitude of characteristics and interests. There is no specific personality or style of being: they come in all different shapes and sizes. They tend to have the strengths of both masculine and feminine characteristics. They can be aggressive and nurturing, sensitive and rigid, dominant and submissive, altruistic and competitive.

Inventive people are introvert and extrovert both—introverts while they develop their ideas and work at excavating related and known facts from different sources, and then extroverts in the presentation, sharing and implementation of their ideas to the larger community. They tend to be good listeners, developing and expressing their ideas well.

Ingenious individuals have a distinctive *ensign*—they have a clear sense of identity and tend to be rebellious and independent. They generally have a well-elevated *crow's nest* and are aware of every aspect of themselves. They consciously or unconsciously develop both the strong and the weak sides of their personalities. They manage to be naïve and streetwise simultaneously and without cynicism. They aim for a sense of completeness.

Imaginative folk have a strong and well-balanced *mast*, and they are generally modest and self-assured. Their *sails* are fully extended as they resourcefully harness every personal ability and opportunity in their environment. When it comes to work, they are extremely self-disciplined and tenacious. They are persistent and full of drive, determination and resolve and they have the ability to concentrate their energy for a long period of time on a particular issue. Their brilliance shows in how they act on new ideas and insights.

Creative people have insatiable curiosity; they are open-minded, flexible, imaginative and adventurous in choosing their destinations. This results in their being receptive to experiencing extremes without personal inner tension or conflict. Ingenious people constantly use their *helm*. They openly explore the interest and enjoyment of life by having a fluid attention and consistently processing events occurring in their environment. They are versatile and easily adaptable to new situations.

Creative people are in control of their *rudder*—in tune with their emotional selves and paying attention to their feelings and intuition. Often sensitive, they are equally as affected by suffering and pain as by joy and ecstasy. They can retreat into a fantasy world and explore as a child. They can be playful and childlike and excited about life. They can be curious and playful to the brink of irresponsibility.

Generally, inventive people are not image-oriented. Their clothes and surroundings reflect who they are and are easy to wear and maintain. Successful creative individuals have a solid, cohesive *hull*. They are extremely honest and true to themselves and their beliefs.

Honesty and integrity are typical hallmarks of creative people. They focus on problems that negatively affect the harmony of the environment or a domain of knowledge. Often they have experienced a difficult or traumatic event in their lives, which has encouraged them to look deep within themselves and to question the accepted social order. They create inventive and brilliant insights to satisfy the gaps that they have identified.

10.1 Activity: Select a Dimension of Your Life for Added Creativity

In your journey so far, you have explored a number of different dimensions of your life, such as sense of self, health, nutrition, communication, conflict resolution, and setting and achieving goals. Within these, there are many other facets—for example, your home environment, garden, cooking, and clothes—that provide ample opportunity for you to expand your creativity and enrich your life. Think about an aspect of your life that you would like to brighten and spice up a little (or a lot!).

Integration Wheel

In your journal note the following:

- What dimension or aspect of your life are you exploring?
- How do you think you may like to be more actively creative?
- Who could you use as a resource and with whom could you share the experience?
- How could you celebrate your new knowledge/growth?

For example, if the realm is cooking, you could plan to expand the variety of the meals you prepare. You may think of taking a cooking course, buying a new cookbook, going to a specialised market, going to a new restaurant to gain new ideas, or even visiting a new culinary destination—Italy perhaps—to attend a cooking course or simply sample the cuisine in the local markets and trattorias. You could plan the next family birthday around an Italian cooking theme, even going so far as to ask guests to dress in a theme for the occasion.

Researched Characteristics of Creative People

The following is a summary of the research conducted by Csikszentmihaly (1997).

Versatile Destinations

Ingenious and inventive people tend to develop and make their careers, sometimes having a number of them. Their versatility enables them to search actively for a niche or niches in which they can be fully and uniquely themselves, true to nature and their beliefs. They are often forced through circumstances to create a job for themselves and this launches them into new and undiscovered territory.

Creative people usually have a deep knowledge of their field and related fields, constantly updating and expanding their knowledge or field of influence. They understand and accept that this knowledge takes time and dedication to assimilate. They respect the people who came before them and the findings and insights their predecessors provided. Although they work at understanding and building on current concepts and paradigms, they are not afraid to challenge and dispute anything they believe no longer holds true.

Like to Explore Old, New and Unknown resources

Inventive people typically have access to a domain of knowledge both in reading material and influential people working in their field. They try to seek and discover new mentors and ideas. They are open to learning new things and understanding different insights, trying always to combine things in different ways to create a new and comprehensive whole.

Excited by the Prospect of Embarking on an Adventure

Creative people enjoy most elements of their lives—in particular their work, to which they commit long hours. Equally, however, they enjoy breaks, exploring nature or other elements of life. It is during these times of relaxation that new ideas incubate.

Creative people are prepared to take risks. When something does not work, they simply learn from the experience and move on. They are not inhibited by guilt. Typically, they spend their lives doing what they love and find their work exhilarating, anticipating that things will not be perfect at first, but trusting that things will evolve over time. In the interim, they make do with what is available in order to achieve their goal. Equally, they are prepared to abandon what is not good or not working out.

Financially they tend to be secure, so that they are able to focus their energies on their work and are not trying to merely survive. While working, they consciously avoid distractions.

Masters of Their Own Time

Successful creative people live very much in the present. They are masters of their own time and ruthlessly defend it against intrusion and being monopolised by others. Truly innovative ideas take time to develop. Innovative people are prepared to invest the time for their creativity to mature to its full potential. They are not easily thwarted by setbacks and naturally view these to be part of the long-term process of being creative and successful. They incorporate this awareness in their approach to projects—both successes and failures.

Their rhythm of life reflects who they are. They often have unusual working hours and times to rest and relax. Importantly, they structure their time in a harmonious way that best suits who they are and how they work. They do not see time as a cost factor. They forget time and simply focus wholly on the task at hand. They become almost unaware of time in their absorption in the task at hand. Events and achievements that occurred in the past do not hamper them.

They have hectic schedules and work long hours, but these periods are interspersed with creative relaxation, doing things they enjoy and find energising. Creativity happens when doing a exercise rather than sitting still and watching. Activities typically linked to creativity include:

- regular walking
- running
- swimming
- driving
- yoga
- taking a long shower

Creative people also make time to develop a valuable network of associates and friends who help support and validate their work.

10.2 Activity: Develop a SMART Goal

> Develop a SMART goal (specific, measurable, achievable, resourced/reasonable, time managed) toward achieving the dimension of your life in which you would like to improve your creativity. Make a note in your journal of your goal and plan.

Seek and Attract Fellow Companions

Innovative people tend to choose to spend their time with people who are positive and congenial, equally interested in and fascinated by the intricacies of life. They have friends from many different walks of life, cultures, and age groups. They like to meet with bright minds. They tend to create supportive groups of people who nurture who they are.

They tend to have long, stable, peaceful and satisfying relationships. Their spouses are often not creative but respect and value their partners' talents. These spouses support them emotionally and physically by providing a stable and congenial environment in which they are able to flourish and fully develop their brilliance by focusing on their work. Creative men are often deeply involved with their families. In the case of divorce, the divorce is usually amicable, with the couple maintaining real friendship after the separation.

Creative people habitually seek out mentors and associates they trust to validate and enhance their ideas and help develop them further. They generally have access to masters in their fields. They speak their minds and defend their points of view adamantly. They often do not do what is expected of them socially, and consequently may be viewed as strange and difficult to get along with. They are often misunderstood and found to be on the periphery of a broader social milieu.

Their Motivation Tends to Be Intrinsic

Creative people only ever do work that they enjoy doing. Their motivation is intrinsic. The unknown challenges them. Recognition and money, although appreciated, are not the driving force behind their enterprises. They have a huge amount of resolve to make sense of their world. Generally, it is the process that they find challenging rather than the final, finished product. This is embodied in the words of Naguib Mahfouz, the Egyptian Nobel Prize winner: "I love my work more than I love what it produces. I am dedicated to my work regardless of the consequences."

Creative people feel that their lives and energy levels are under their own control. They often have a low threshold for pain and are easily troubled, as they are unable to ignore things that don't appear to make sense or are unjust and they feel compelled to act. They have a positive disposition, and although they are passionate about their work, they maintain the ability to be objective and open to new and differing elements. They seek and accept constructive criticism and response. Their ego does not inhibit their focus or attitude. They are known for their endurance, perseverance and general dedication to hard work.

Surroundings Are Meaningful

Creative people like to live and work in environments that reflect their uniqueness. They create environments that are meaningful for them and accommodate their sense of time and space. They like to be in a harmonious atmosphere—a place that helps them extend current ideas and generate new ones—and they prefer familiar and comfortable surroundings. They are often found working in beautiful and tranquil settings, being close to nature and collecting interesting things that are meaningful to them. They surround themselves with items that validate who they are or who they aspire to be, having their own space that is tailor-made to their particular needs.

Often they like to visit contrasting environments, enjoying situations that have great activity and then retreating to places that are peaceful, calm, and beautiful. Creativity appears to be nurtured in ambiguous or cross-cultural environments. Creative people are often from a mixed cultural background or have lived in different cultures or cross-cultural settings.

10.3 Activity: Creating an Ideal Creative Environment

Below is a list of attributes that are typical of the habits and environment in which creative and innovative people immerse themselves. In your journal, note the degree to which these attributes are represented in your life. Now, consider the impact if you were to consciously incorporate them into your lifestyle. How would they enable you to be more creative? Habits and attributes typical of creative people include:

- having clear goals every step of the way
- setting goals that are attainable in easily achievable steps
- gaining immediate feedback about the success of actions taken
- balancing between ability in skills and the presented challenge
- living in a supportive and congenial environment
- having no concerns as to the consequences of failure
- working in a competitive and supportive environment
- keeping distractions to a minimum
- encouraging an element of fun
- having access to the latest innovations in the field
- having access to the best technology and equipment
- having access to significant colleagues and masters in the field
- walking for exercise/fitness
- running for exercise/fitness
- swimming for exercise/fitness
- driving for pleasure
- taking long showers

Thinking Intelligence

Although creative people are intelligent, they are often not recognised for their intellectual ability at school. However, they tend to have a high ability to concentrate and focus on tasks. They generally have good inductive as well as deductive reasoning skills. They are convergent and divergent thinkers, with good judgment and the ability to recognise a problem. They trust and act on their intuition. Innovative people have a vision as to what will become important in the future and are able to select good ideas to develop from a group of possible projects. They tap into whatever sources are available.

Awareness of Global Issues

Creative people often have a sense of global awareness and are searching for solutions that will positively solve the world's problems. They are often found doing altruistic work, particularly later in life. They tend to be quite idealistic and like to address global issues of environmental deterioration and poverty. Generally they are anti-war and anti-violence. Although they are aware of the enormity of the world's problems, they tackle finding solutions to them in a light-hearted manner and are not depressive in their view of the world or in their work.

10.4 Activity: Stretching Your Creativity

Looking at the chart "Characteristics Typical of Creative People," note the ambiguity of the characteristics included. Circle in green those characteristics that are typical of you and in yellow those you would like to further develop or integrate into your life.

Characteristics Typical of Creative People

many interests	rigid	amicable surroundings
clear sense of identity	dominant	good expression
honest and with integrity	not image-oriented	naïve
follows a natural rhythm	submissive	streetwise
spiritually aware	altruistic	not cynical
modest	competitive	rebellious
self-assured	introvert/extrovert	independent
aggressive	considered unique	playful/excited
nurturing	a good listener	no inner tension
sensitive listens to feelings	enjoys congenial people	goal-orientated
no guilt	positive disposition	interested in life
sensitive to joyfulness	plays hard	energetic
sensitive to pain	proactive	spends time in nature
spontaneous	access to people and resources	idealistic
follows intuition	manages time	invests time in self
expands knowledge	on the fringe of the	totally committed
hardworking/patient	larger group	motivated by challenge
values amicable	desire to solve global problems	not motivated by money
relationships	seeks to understand from	long-standing friendships
	every perspective	takes risks
	respectful	

꩜ *10.5 Activity: Stretching Your Creativity*

In your journal, note how you intend to develop the above. For the characteristics circled in yellow, consider how you will develop or integrate them into your life and how this will stretch your creativity. Also reflect on the ones you circled in green and how these already enrich your life.

The Creative Model as Developed from Csikszentmihaly's Research

The following are the steps (though not always strictly adhered to) that creative people typically follow:

1. *Prepare.* Become immersed in a particular domain, acquiring a high degree of knowledge, skill and fundamental know-how in the field and related areas.
2. *Question.* Challenge anything that does not fully explain the current paradigm or contradicts another paradigm.
3. *Think, think, think!*
4. *Allow an idle incubation period.* Ideas often appear to develop in the subconscious, coming to the fore in dreams and on waking from a deep sleep. New ideas rarely develop in a linear fashion, but are rather a product of the combination of a number of concepts in different levels or relationships to each other.
5. *Have an insight.* The "Aha!" experience.
6. *Evaluate the idea.* Is it viable? Is it worth pursuing?
7. *Recognise the opportunity.* See the potential to implement the concept in the present context of knowledge or apply it outside to other domains.
8. *Evaluate.* Test the idea on valued friends and colleagues, being open to constructive criticism and input.
9. *Work, work, work!*
10. *Develop.* Elaborate and develop the idea further.

 10.6 Activity: Where to Now?

In your journal, draw a picture of where you would like to be in the future, using colour to reflect how you feel about these future possibilities.

In essence, I have been encouraging you to explore your potential. Recognised innovative people have a definite disposition: they have strong clear values and a clear sense of identity. They have an accurate awareness of their emotions and a keen rational ability. They plan and know the direction in which they want to go and are dedicated to the task of getting there. They have an unobstructed vision and are easily able to look objectively at who they are and where they stand in relation to those around them.

They have a deep knowledge of their specific domain and the current agreed and recognised paradigms in their field. Simultaneously, they manage their time, stress and general all-round health in a positive and effective manner. They live a balanced and healthy lifestyle in every element of their experience.

Being recognised and successful is in part a combination of all or some of the above elements, but it is also partly due to the luck of being born into the ideal circumstances and being in the right place at the right time with the right idea. It also requires meeting the right people who can recognise the opportunity or idea as valuable and can help to give it credence and make it available to a wider audience.

Craig Ballantyne

Most creative people have a belief system that accepts and respects all religions. Typically, they have a true and deep spiritual awareness that there is a force greater than man and his abilities, and a belief that this is the source of their creative spirit. We will visit this dimension in the final leg of our journey.

We all have the potential to be more creative in our own lives and in our realm of influence. There is no magic formula. It simply takes the desire and the application. In the following chapter, we are going to explore creativity in terms of your sensuality and sexuality.

CHAPTER 11
Sensuality by the Light of the Moon

Song of Songs

How beautiful your sandaled feet,
O prince's daughter!
Your graceful legs are like jewels, the work of an artist's hands.
Your navel is a rounded goblet that never lacks blended wine.
Your waist is a mound of wheat encircled by lilies.
Your breasts are like two fawns, like twin fawns of a gazelle.
Your neck is like an ivory tower.
Your eyes are the pools of Heshbon by the gate of Bath Rabbim.
Your nose is like the tower of Lebanon looking toward Damascus.
Your head crowns you like Mount Carmel.
Your hair is like royal tapestry; the king is held captive by its tresses.
How beautiful you are and how pleasing, my love, with your delights!
Your stature is like that of the palm, and your breasts like clusters of fruit.
I said, "I will climb the palm tree; I will take hold of its fruit."
May your breasts be like clusters of grapes on the vine, the fragrance of your
breath like apples, and your mouth like the best wine.

May the wine go straight to my beloved, flowing gently over lips and teeth.
I belong to my beloved, and his desire is for me.
Come, my beloved, let us go to the countryside, let us spend the night in the villages.
Let us go early to the vineyards to see if the vines have budded, if their blossoms
have opened, and if the pomegranates are in bloom— there I will give you my love.
The mandrakes send out their fragrance, and at our door is every delicacy, both
new and old, that I have stored up for you, my beloved.

—Song of Solomon 7:1, New International Version

Itinerary

We are going to reflect on how your sensuality is embodied in every dimension of your life, in how you express yourself with particular focus on the "special other," and in how the two of you relate.

Viewpoints

Sensuality encompasses all of the viewpoints included in this journey.

Travel Bag

You will need:
- Relaxing music
- Massage oil
- Towels and blankets
- Candles
- Bubble bath
- Sexy clothes
- Allocated time
- Safe private place
- Partner or play mate!

Introduction

The topic of sensuality provides an excellent opportunity to summarise all of the content discussed so far. Sensuality is a factor that encompasses every dimension of our lives and is not limited to the act of sex alone. If explored to its full potential, it encompasses all of the viewpoints that were identified at the start of this journey. It is about our mind, body and soul; and it provides us with the opportunity to bring all of our senses together.

The Ancient Greeks talked of three types of love: *Agape*, which is the unconditional love one can have for another; *Eros*, the love of passion and fusion; and *Philia*, the brotherly love of time spent together in mutual support and interest. A healthy sensual and sexual relationship with the "special other" in your life is a balance of all of these. Attaining this balance takes ongoing commitment and effort. In this chapter, we will reflect on each of these with a special focus on sensuality in relationship to the special other.

Sex encompasses many things. It is how we interweave the special other into every dimension of our lives. It is the quiet look across the room, the love note on the pillow, the flowers on the breakfast table, nurturing gestures, the affectionate kiss as we go out the door, the laughter in the night. It takes the conscious commitment of time to focus on our needs and those of the other and to weave this in a sensitive, nurturing and connected manner into the routine and meaning of our lives.

Sensuality in Relation to Your Sailing Craft

Sensuality is a veil that potentially adorns you and your partner's sailing craft. The physical act of sex provides an opportunity for intimacy, physical expression and procreation. The *keel* illustrates our sense of purpose and, in this instance, our commitment to the special other in our lives.

The *hull* depicts how we enjoy and express this, which is strongly influenced by our and the other's values and beliefs. What are these, where did they come from and how do they reflect who we are today? Are they representative of a time long ago and reflective of another's values and belief system? Have we developed our own individual worldview in relation to this subject, or are we holding on to those of our parents or the community in which we were raised or live?

The *rudder* portrays our emotional awareness, which plays a vital role in determining our mood and how we constructively connect to the other's emotions and sense of fun and adventure. The *mast* represents our self-esteem and plays an enormous role in providing the confidence to explore and ask for what we need for our partner and ourselves. A high level of self-esteem allows us to discover, love and appreciate our bodies' potential for sensuality.

The *sails* provide a canvas on which to analyse our and our partner's motivation for connection and sexual expression. Motivation with respect to sensuality is complex, on an individual level, couple level and within the broader social context. If we refer back to Maslow's hierarchy of needs, the initial sex drive is present in the lower order physical needs, followed by the impulse for safety and security in terms of place, health and hygiene and protective practice from unwanted pregnancies and sexually transmitted diseases.

Following this is the yearning for social connection. Sensual expression provides the opportunity to share with another and be affirmed for who we are. It provides a social opportunity to recognise and honour the relationship, leading to a sense of fulfilment.

The social context and culture in which we live will also have a profound affect on how we feel and act around the concept of sensuality. Our demonstrated sensuality also can reflect our sense of power and status. Finally, the sense of completeness as described as self-actualisation can be potentially experienced in a fully satisfying relationship.

The unfurling of the sails reminds us of the need to be giving and receiving in our sensuality. Is there a commitment to ensure mutual satisfaction and pleasure? The *helm* reminds us of the need to be constantly exploring what is enriching and what is not, and how to sustain a sense of freshness and novelty to ensure that both parties' needs and desires are met in mutually beneficial ways.

The *crow's nest* provides our worldview. Are we open to other expressions of sexuality? Are we willing to explore other territories in a mature and trusting fashion? Are we our own person, and are we fully independent emotionally, cognitively and financially? Our sexual life ideally should be a reflection of who we are or aspire to be.

Our cargo includes both real and imagined hurts that may limit and inhibit us in our connection with our special other. Incidents of emotional, sexual and physical abuse may mar our current experience consciously and unconsciously. Our *compass* guides us in providing a moral grounding in all of our sexual expression.

11.1 Activity: Draw a Sensual Sailing Craft

Draw a sailing craft reflecting your and your partner's sexual perspectives. Include in your journal any insights that you may have gained.

Pillow Talk: Communication and Connection

With respect to the transactional-analysis model, mature sex asks us what are our values and beliefs and where have they developed from. With the use of our Adult we can explore if they are relevant today and appropriate to our current relationship. By exploring these fully with our partner and ourselves, we have the opportunity to expand our Johari arena window for our partner and ourselves. Sharing what is enjoyable and what is not, plays an important part in building an understanding of what creates a successful sensual outcome. For example, sharing a sexual fantasy can enrich an experience by creating a privately shared world.

Transactional Analysis with Respect to Sensuality

Positive Parent: The Positive Parent provides the beliefs and values and how we appreciate and respect our own body and that of the other person. It is what we bring to any encounter with another person. The Positive Parent holds our moral standard, something to be explored prior to an encounter. Our family of origin has helped form this view of the world and our history, which ideally has then been explored, pruned and consciously formulated. It includes things like integrity, congruence, transparency, and trust. It also holds the conscious decision to commit to another person. Non-commitment to an intimate relationship potentially leaves us lonelier than ever. Without an intimate relationship, sensual pleasuring quickly becomes boring and unfulfilling.

Negative Parent: The Negative Parent will set the boundaries for what is healthy and appropriate for the individual. These need to be thought through ahead of time. The physical needs of the body can very easily cloud the rational part of the brain if not enhanced and schooled beforehand. And even then, not always. We also may want to let go of any need to be in control and simply abandon ourselves to the experience.

Double Negative Parent: Is there an underlying manipulative Negative Parent that is critical, judging and controlling? All these factors contribute to poor sexual fulfilment. Where sex is demanded, coerced, and used to harm, manipulate, or exercise power over the other, that is evidence of a Double Negative Parent. In these instances, no matter how subtle, it is abuse. Abusive sex leaves scars.

The Adult is our fact-finding aspect of understanding, reasoning and information-gathering. This is where we use our inner scientist and Socratic questions of what, where, how, which, when, and whom. The Adult directs our thinking and decisions. It is the Adult who acquires the knowledge and understanding of how the different parts of the body work and how these need to be accommodated in order to reach maximum satisfaction for both parties. The Adult also develops a responsible, mature and rational approach to exploring and ensuring that the time and actions occur in a healthy and safe context.

With the Adult, we set the boundaries for our sensual activities. We need to engage the Adult in order to plan and prepare for quality time, space and creative resources for the special other and ourselves, to be able to express our mutual sexual needs and desires. Ironically, we need to plan for fun.

Positive Child: The playful enthusiasm and inspiration of the Positive Child plays a very important role in healthy sensual pleasure. It provides the possibility of viewing sensual expression as an ongoing adventure. The individual's Positive Child is creative and humorous in its approach to sharing pleasure in a fun, trusting and lively manner. The Positive Child also holds the lovely sense of warmth and glow, peace, calm and serenity after a fulfilling encounter.

Negative Child: The Negative Child may potentially be concerned with inhibitions, shame and performance anxiety. Covert Negative Child's emotions of anxiety, fear, guilt and boredom, and Overt Negative Child's emotions of anger, irritation, disappointment, hostility, disrespect and negativity, all sabotage attempts to achieve intimacy and orgasm.

11.2 Activity: Explore Your Sensuality in Terms of TA

Using your Adult explore your attitude to sensuality:

- How, when and where did I get my sexual knowledge?
- How old was I?
- What impact did this have on me?
- What does the act of sensual expression mean to me?
- What do I know about the physical elements of my body and my partner's?
- What were my parents' and significant others' attitude to sex?
- How has this impacted on my own views?
- Do these need to be reflected upon?
- When should I be prepared to have a sexual encounter with another?
- What do I want from sex?
- How can I express this?
- What is being romantic?

In your current approach to sensual fulfilment, how are the following demonstrated?

Positive Parent

Negative Parent

Double Negative Parent

Positive Child

Negative Child—Overt

Negative Child—Covert

We need to be open to continually learning and incorporating new ideas and challenging old and staid ones. Men and women are wired differently. Good sensual pleasuring is about creating a win–win for both parties involved. Fantasies should include your partner and should not involve pain or domination. Open communication is essential to enable healthy adjustments to increase greater mutual sensual pleasure. It means talking about sex and creating a set of verbal and non-verbal cues that express what you are feeling and affirm your shared experience.

Expressing your sensuality and sexuality is not about technique but rather about attitude and energy and how to connect with the other in a mutually empowering manner.

11.3 Activity: Enhancing Your Expression

Consider which of the following you could include to enhance your sensual expression in relation to your special Other. Sensual pleasure needs to be on the priority list!

- planning for the intimate time together
- enlisting all the senses—touch, smell, taste, sound and sight
- resolving past conflicts and hurts
- planning date nights
- ensuring a private secure place—lock the door!
- planned vacations
- hiring a babysitter
- being open to a "quickie"
- watching a sensual movie
- turning off the TV and the phone
- planning to be sexy
- engaging in mutual sexual fantasy
- being fit and healthy—sexy no matter what age
- variety of activities—dancing, massage, showers, dinners out, weekend away, talk, and fantasy

- using props—mirrors, music, clothes, oils, lotions, sexy clothes, lingerie, pillows
- engaging all parts of your body
- bubble bath
- going nude
- using a special perfume
- being creative through fantasy and action
- nurturing attitude
- daily commitment to connection
- safe haven
- variety
- fun clothes and supports
- being open to new positions
- candles
- creating a romantic atmosphere conducive to play in each other's garden
- making love under the stars

Physical Dimensions of Sex

It is not the purpose of this book to unpack the physical mechanics of sex and orgasm. However, if you are experiencing difficulty in this area of your life, it is recommended that you seek out appropriate literature in order to enhance your knowledge. Sexual experiences are a complex relationship of nerves, hormones, muscles and blood vessels, as well as mental attitude and energy and context. In order for an individual to climax, both the parasympathetic and sympathetic nervous system must be involved.

We need to be assertive in our approach. We need to create the time, space and sense of security necessary to have good sex. Part of this is having the right attitude and expectancy, and expressing our needs so as to allow and enable our partner to provide what we desire and yearn for. It is our responsibility to understand our own sexual needs and to create the space, attitude, and expectation for this to occur. We need to be open to experiencing a healthy sexual encounter and acknowledge and allow our partner to enable us to achieve this. Healthy sensual pleasuring occurs where there is a win–win for both parties. In case of conflicts, there is a commitment to resolve these productively and in a timely way, through the making of a daily commitment to honour the other.

Barriers to Intimacy

- *Physical differences:* Females and males are physically different and function and climax very differently, with many woman having the ability to experience multiple climaxes but generally requiring a longer period for arousal, while men tend to be able experience one significant orgasm quickly and need a longer period of time before they can climax a second time. There are four phases: excitement, plateau, orgasm(s) and resolution. By extending and relishing the time of the first, second and final stages, the opportunity grows to build and increase the intimacy of the relationship.

- *Objectifying the act of sex:* This factor is often insidious and subliminally toxic. It generally includes an adulterous focus of attention elsewhere, whether it be an affair (real or imagined), work, children, friends, or pornography. It also includes a conscious or unconscious intention to control or manipulate the other. Objectifying sex potentially allows it to become an addiction.

- *Poor body image:* A poor body image is a reflection of a strong and unhelpful Negative Parent and Negative Child. These beliefs and thoughts require exploration and eradication.

- *Stressors:* Stress by its very nature weakens the quality of, and the opportunities and desire for intimacy. Similarly, being physical healthy and fit are factors that increase one's attractiveness to the other and one's physical ability and appetite for sex.

- *Time and financial management:* Simply put, an undisciplined lifestyle leads to poor sensual pleasure. To fully achieve sensual pleasure, one needs to have the resources and security to sustain a physical intimate relationship.

11.4 Activity: Identifying Barriers

Reflect in your journal about any barriers to intimacy that exist for you and your partner.

Introducing Creativity, Spontaneity, and Novelty

Sexuality is like a dance whereby we jointly and creatively develop a sequence of steps and movements that bring us to a mutually enjoyable climax. However, if we were to perform the same steps and rhythm repeatedly, the dance would become boring and lose its appeal and sense of pleasure and enjoyment. To avoid this, we need to consciously create new ways to embellish and create and explore new dances together. This subtlety and variety will help to ensure a lifelong enjoyment and celebration of mutual sexual expression and enjoyment. The new dances need to be choreographed with varying tempos, rhythms, and moods. In essence, this need for variety of expression has been explored in how we engage our taste buds and nurture our bodies.

Enjoyable lifelong sexual encounters call for variety and adaptability in a healthy, energetic and creative manner. This includes fantasy, expression of emotions, open communication, aesthetics, commitment, and time and space. Areas of conflict and dissatisfaction need to be explored, understood, and resolved. As with any tensions, the sooner the better! Guide your partner into what you find to be pleasurable and satisfying. This may even require you to demonstrate what is pleasurable for you.

11.5 Activity: Characteristics of Healthy Sexual Expression

Which of the characteristics below do you currently bring to your relationship with the special other in your life? What would you like to add?

Open	Honest
Respectful	Mutual
Playful	Passionate
Romantic	Quick
Slow	Hard
Fast	Giving
Receiving	Leading
Serving	Exploring
Humour	Laughter
Playful	Adaptive
Assertive	Flexible
Unpredictable	Considerate
Emotional	Serene

Massage

Massage provides the opportunity to curiously explore and excite the special other's erogenous zones in a creative and caring manner. Massage takes the focus off performance. There are many wonderful resources on this topic, which you are encouraged to research and explore. Below is a brief suggested outline on how to nurture and caress your partner's body.

- Ensure that both of you are comfortable. A blanket-covered dining-room table can provide the right height so that the person providing the massage is not cramped or uncomfortable. Ensure that the table is sturdy enough for this activity.
- Put on relaxing music and dim the lights. Creating a safe atmosphere with the help of these and other props will allow a sense of relaxation to occur and thereby enhance the experience for both of you. Cover the person to create a sense of safety and security, only exposing the part of the body you are currently massaging.
- The person providing the massage needs to commit to allowing time and not rushing the process, actively exploring the arousal of the other while containing his or her own. A mindful and focused approach allows for the building of anticipation of reaching a heightened physical experience.
- Focus on the pleasure of being together rather than the final climax.
- Give yourself, the person providing the massage, permission and time to enjoy the journey.

- Use lotion to assist the flow of movement over the body and to bring in the sense of smell. There are a variety of massage oils—including coconut, sesame-seed, almond, and avocado—and some are deliciously scented. Warm the oil first by placing it on your palms and vigorously rubbing your hands together. Be careful not to apply too much.
- Monitor your breathing, taking deep smooth breaths so as to increase the sense of calm and peace.
- Different parts of the body have varying degrees of sensitivity, and it is suggested that you start at the less sensual parts of the body and gradually move toward the more sensitive. This approach builds stimulation and anticipation.
- The entire body is a network of sensory stimulation. In your touch, be creative in varying the type of stroke and pressure applied—sometimes soft, sometimes hard, moving in a variety of different directions, sometimes moving the skin together, sometimes apart.
- Ensure your partner is comfortable and feels safe and warm. Frequently ask for affirmation and guidance on what is pleasurable and enriching and what is not.
- Caress arms, shoulders, outer ears and earlobes, scalp, chest, buttocks and calves, back of knees, inner thighs, armpits, abdomen, small of back, neck, palms of hands, bottom of feet, face, eyelids, nose, temple, and mouth.
- Use differing parts of your body to apply stimulation to your partner: fingertips, palms of hands, elbows, feet, eyelashes, lips, tongue.
- In time, move toward more erotic sensual areas, and then move away to create a sense of excitement and anticipation.
- Be mysterious, tantalizing, and surprising, varying your stroke and pressure. Move from the general to the specific in a leisurely fashion.
- Sex is not clean and orderly. Plan for that so as to minimize embarrassment or discomfort to both parties involved. Keep a box of tissues or a small towel handy.

11.6 Activity: Give Each Other a Massage

On different occasions, take turns giving each other a special massage dedicated solely to the pleasuring of the other. Reflect in your journal on your experience giving and receiving a massage, and share with your partner any insights you may have had.

11.7 Activity: How Could You Expand Your Sensual Expression?

Select your least-developed sense and think how you could introduce a new way of being in your lovemaking and intimate relationship. How would you create your perfect love nest?

Occasional sexual dysfunction is normal, especially if it can be explained within the context of relationship or context stressors. However, if it persists, you are encouraged to seek the help of a professional.

Good sex encompasses mind, body and spirit. It extends from a strong embrace to a gentle hand-holding, from joyful tears to open nakedness and a hidden and seductive mystery. Our bodies are sacred and it therefore follows that any form of sexual expression that can either enhance our general sense of spiritual well-being or diminish it. This brings us to our final chapter on spirituality.

CHAPTER 12
The Compass: Our Moral and Spiritual Guide

Illusions

Once there lived a village of creatures along the bottom of a great crystal river.

The current of the river swept silently over them all—young and old, rich and poor, good and evil, the current going its own way, knowing its own crystal self.

Each creature in its own manner clung tightly to the twigs and rocks of the river bottom, for clinging was their way of life, and resisting the current what each had learned from birth.

But one creature said at last, "I am tired of clinging. Though I cannot see it with my eyes, I trust that the current knows where it is going. I shall let go, and let it take me where it will. Clinging I shall die of boredom!"

The other creatures laughed and said, "Fool! Let go, and that current you worship will throw you tumbled and smashed across the rocks, and you will die quicker than boredom!"

But the one heeded them not, and taking a breath, did let go, and at once was tumbled and smashed by the current across the rocks.

Yet in time, as the creature refused to cling again, the current lifted him free from the bottom, and he was bruised and hurt no more.

And the creatures downstream, to whom he was a stranger, cried "See a miracle! A creature like ourselves, yet he flies! See the Messiah come to save us all!"

And the one carried in the current said, "I am no more messiah than you. The river delights to lift us free, if only we dare let go. Our true work is this voyage, this adventure."

But they cried the more, "Savior!" All the while clinging to the rocks, and when they looked again he was gone, and they were left alone making legends of a Savior.

—Richard Bach

Itinerary

In this chapter, you will integrate the territory explored to date into a uniquely personal spiritual perspective.

Viewpoint

The focus will be on spirituality.

Travel Bag

You will need:
- a quiet, private place to meditate and contemplate a poem or a spiritual book
- access to the Internet
- your journal

Introduction

This chapter is a synthesis of all that we have examined and explored in your journey to a new horizon. The purpose and destination of this guide was to make you, the traveller, more conscious of your own unique place in the universe—in essence, more conscious of your spirituality.

Spirituality encompasses all things; it is our keel, our ballast, the essence from which our beliefs and values are reflected in the lives that we live. It is our unique and personal view of the universe in which we are immersed. It is a synthesis of all that has gone before and the foundation of all that will follow. Every thought and action in every moment of our day reflects it.

Ideally, our spiritual belief system is something we have contemplated deeply. It is the reflection of our carnal self and our divine potential. It provides meaning to our existence and locates us, directing our activities in life-serving ways.

Jung suggests that, just as we have animal instincts, we also have spiritual instincts that drive us toward a sense of connectedness with something greater than ourselves. He proposes that it is through this connection that we ourselves are transformed into something greater. It allows for meaning to be found in all life experiences, making even the most painful bearable and meaningful. He goes on to equate an absence of meaning with illness.

With the expansion of science, traditional religions have lost their foothold and power. However, science does not provide a sense of spiritual meaning. This is evident in the increasing levels of depression and suicide in developed and developing communities, where ideologies of immediate gratification, materialism and hedonism have been embraced.

With the waning of traditional religions, there has been a rise in the social sciences and the field of new-age thinking and psychology. Jung believes this development to be a natural compensation for the loss of traditional forms of faith. He suggests our spiritual instincts have led us to develop concepts that can replace what traditional beliefs and mythologies provided. It is an attempt to provide a positive linkage between ourselves and nature and the wider cosmos, a way to locate ourselves in the larger community.

According to Jung, this instinct is within each one of us. For us to discover and own authentic meaning we need to search and explore ancient myths and practices, dreams and religions. These will provide insights and a guide to our own spiritual journey within. However, for many, the traditional religions still provide a sense of belonging and tenure.

12.1 Activity: *Consider How You Would Like to Be Remembered.*

Take a moment to think about how you would like to be remembered. What would you like to hear from your authentic pulse within? Write down your thoughts in your journal.

Human Beings: A Reflection of the Carnal and the Divine

The term *human being* depicts the complexity of our nature. *Human* reflects our instinctive carnal behaviour. Our instincts have ensured our survival to date and include our nurturing, territorial and procreational behaviour. In balance, our instincts help to ensure our survival as individuals and as a species.

These reflexive instincts are housed in the reptilian part of our brain. Our rational cognitive ability in the more evolved cerebral brain allows us the opportunity, through choice, to rise above the immediate instinctive drives. It gives us the capacity to think and act in a responsible manner. By using this part of our brain, we can move toward a greater awareness of our bodies, our instincts, and our drives. By being aware, we can enhance and direct our energy toward more consciously chosen behaviour.

This raised level of consciousness also creates a bridge between our carnality and our *being*, our spiritual self. With this awareness comes the evolution and acceptance that there is something greater than ourselves, the insight that we are an infinitely small part of a universe that is expansive in time and space.

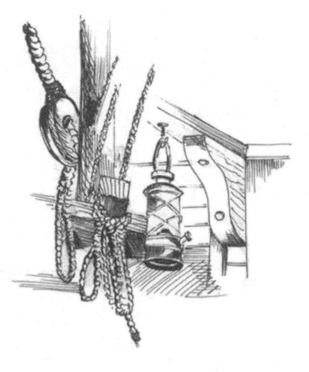

✆ *12.2 Activity: Our Place in the Universe*

Take the time to search the Internet for the structure and makeup of a single cell of an animal or plant. Look at the sky on a clear night and scan the vastness of the universe. Become aware of the complexity, beauty and intricacy of what we call our universe. It can be a very humbling experience. Know that to understand it all is beyond any of our current potential. Yet the very fact that we are able to view and witness it all makes us an integral part of this amazing whole. Once you have done this, reflect in your journal how you feel about your place in the universe and how it has changed during your journey of self-discovery.

Increasing and fine-tuning our conscious awareness of our place in this marvellous mystery allows us the opportunity to participate in it more fully and deeply, and to acknowledge our full carnal and angelic potential. As we expand our awareness, we become more and more conscious that everything is linked and part of one creation. There are no dividing lines.

Every action and non-action has a consequence and a repercussion in the greater scheme of life. It is in recognising our interconnectedness with all things that we are simultaneously humbled and exalted. With a heightened awareness, we can begin to take responsibility for each of our actions, knowing of their impact on the greater whole. This concept is termed the *butterfly effect*.

The Butterfly Effect

I remember reading a science-fiction short story as a school text many years ago. I forget the title or the author, but it illustrated the concept of the butterfly effect beautifully. The story started with a small group of people waiting to go on a safari in a time machine to the age of the dinosaurs. The tour operator had previewed the experience to ensure that as time naturally unfolded, none of the tourists would interfere with the previous reality.

As the group waited for their time machine to be prepared, they discussed the outcome of the recent national election. The outcome of the narrowly won battle was that the good guys had won the election and thereby saved the globe from disaster. The election results were displayed on the front page of a newspaper visible on a stand near the door of the time machine.

At the designated time and with much excitement, the group entered the time machine and were given strict instructions to stay on the paths suspended above the forest floor, thus ensuring that their visit would have no impact on the course of history. Miraculously, the group arrived in the time of dinosaurs and started to explore the jungle on the suspended paths.

As planned, they encountered a group of dinosaurs. The enormity and terror of the scene caused one of the members to panic and inadvertently step off the path—and in her flurry accidentally crush a small butterfly. The sightseers innocently believed that the premature death of a single butterfly could not possibly ricochet through the course of time and have any impact, and therefore they kept the event to themselves.

On their return, the exhilarated travellers were astonished to be greeted by a slightly altered scene. Nothing was quite the same; things were a bit less organised, dustier, the form of the letters bearing the daily news slightly changed. But most importantly, the result of the election was reversed. The *bad* guys had won. The story, as I remember, leaves the group in stunned silence.

This universal awareness of the interconnectedness of all things is reflected in the belief and social systems of many "primitive" native tribes. In the book *The Lost World of the Kalahari* (2010), Laurens van der Post describes the traditions and beliefs of the Bushman people living in the Kalahari Desert. These nomadic people live in clans and have survived in one of the world's harshest environments. Their survival can be attributed to their close attunement to their environment, the seasons and one another.

Their survival as a clan was dependent on how carefully and purely they managed the ecological system of which they were an integral part. For example, when harvesting tubers from the ground, where there were three, they would harvest only one, leaving the remaining two to reproduce and be available for harvest in another season, possibly by another clan. Taking note that their environment could only support so many human beings, they practiced birth control through abstinence. They kept their numbers within the range that the desert could support and feed. The clan would discuss when a new member could be added and which family would be given the opportunity to have a child.

Likewise, when conflicts occurred between the clans or within the clan, the communities affected would sit and discuss the problem until a viable solution was found for all parties involved. Disputes were seldom settled violently, as it was viewed that human beings were too precious to be damaged in this manner. They nurtured their young and old, allowing them a dignified death when they were no longer able to keep up with the nomadic life of the clan. They cherished their culture through song, dance, and storytelling, and recorded their lives in artworks in their cave dwellings. All this—and yet they have been labelled *primitive*! We need to rediscover this "aware" *primitive* self and bring it into harmony with our surroundings, one another and the world at large.

The reality is that we are all interconnected, down to the most miniscule scale. This is apparent with the range, scope and impact of our latest technological advances, in particular the Internet. Every thought, word and deed impacts on us and those around us and so continues to ripple out to the universe.

This awareness of our interconnectedness and the responsibility that goes with it would translate into a very different global paradigm if consciously applied in our lives. It would change how we manage our involvement in business operations and the environment. *Aware* businesses would take responsibility for the short- and long-term impact of their products—not only for their consumers but also for all global residents and the environment. The cost of the disposal of used and abandoned items would be built into the original cost of the item so that it could be borne by the consumer rather than by the majority, many of whom do not have the resources to partake in the benefit of the original product. Instead, these people are subjected to the by-products—the pollution of its generation and disposal.

Consumerism as we know it today would diminish and finally vanish. Materialism would be understood as a carnal form of power and status identity. Its effect—making the rich richer and the poor poorer—and the negative impact of this on the planet would be understood. The religion of consumerism and materialism would be seen not to hold the promise of long-term global political, social, or environmental stability.

Traditional Philosophies

And what of traditional philosophies? Traditional religion is man's determination to reflect his and the community's divine image. Potentially, it provides the opportunity for the synergy of like-minded souls to meet and expand their awareness. The ritual and the symbolism connect us with something larger than ourselves. They allow us the regular opportunity to pause and think about who we are, our values, image, emotions, motivation and level of self-attunement. They acknowledge rights of passage that confirm the transition from childhood to puberty and then to adulthood. They announce birth and death and the union of two souls. They provide the structure to celebrate and mourn the lives that we live. Ideally, they allow us to harness all that we are and reach our full human potential.

A religious or spiritual group can provide a warm nurturing environment, with a loving and forgiving Positive Parent–style God who engenders a sense of security and engages your Positive Child. Equally, it has the capacity to focus on the negative side of the controlling carnal nature of man. Instead of providing a loving and supportive environment in which to grow, the church or institution becomes a reflection of the Negative Parent. Energy becomes trapped in the convoluted process of bureaucracy, roles, and judgments, causing us to feel fearful and insecure by triggering our Negative Child. Hollis (1993) suggests that if this comes without a sense of "soul," then it is no more than a form of ideology. It is important that we be vigilant and challenge the integrity of any institution with which we choose to associate ourselves.

We need to embrace the concept of traditional religion as a verb, as a way of being rather than as a finite entity or a fixed immovable object. This stance allows us to see our path as one of many—that our path and belief system is of equal value to others' paths and belief systems. Each provides an interpretation and possible sense of the meaning of our place in the universe. By taking this perspective, we allow space for ourselves to be respectful, accepting, and inclusive of our own worldview as it grows and evolves, as well as inclusive of other views of the world. From this perspective, we have the potential to transcend tribal interest and individual self-centeredness. It is only with this inclusive approach to spiritual focus that we can actively work toward a place of world peace and understanding in our increasingly global village.

AMA Samy (2005), a Jesuit priest and Zen master, encourages us to move beyond a fundamentalist religious view. This he calls being "first born," when we see our "way" as the only "way." This type of fundamentalism can occur beyond the realm of religion and is evident in any collection of people who become adamant that theirs is the only way. For example, Marxists, vegetarians and health fanatics also have the potential of being prescriptive and dogmatic in their worldview.

Samy suggests that we should rather move to a place of being "second born," where we accept that there are many authentic ways in which to find spiritual meaning, be it through church, temple, mosque, or yoga practice. For a prosperous global village to become a reality, a cornerstone would be for all to take a stance of tolerance and accommodation of all forms of spirituality and faith.

Fundamentally, all religions advocate loving one another and ourselves. If we could apply this in our lives, in the purest sense, we would resolve many of the world's problems in an amazingly short period of time. A wise Catholic friend of mine, when talking to her new Jewish daughter-in-law about her son's conversion to Judaism, simply said, "I do not mind what religion you follow, my only request is that you practice it in its integrity."

This practice and application of beliefs takes time. We need to regularly allow room in our daily routine to reflect and tune in to our values and beliefs and how we demonstrate them in our lifestyle. We create a spiritual disposition in our lives by being loving and authentic in living and sharing our values, being conscious of and responsible for our emotions, following our intuition, and giving space to our creativity.

12.3 Activity: Exploring Your Perception of "God."

Reflect in your journal your view of "God." Does He/She exist, and if so, does your image portray and reflect a Positive or Negative Parent perspective? How does this view of God support and help you grow as an individual and as a community member? Does it tap into your Positive Child, leaving you feeling secure and loved, or does it engage your Negative Child, promoting a sense of inadequacy, fear and anxiety? If you have developed a moral code outside of that or adopted one from an organisation that you are associated with, how does this support and guide you, and is it adequate?

12.4 Activity: How Would You Like to Be Remembered?

Take a moment and think about how you would like to be remembered. If you could write your own obituary, what would you authentically like to say?

 12.5 Activity: Write Your Own Spiritual Manifesto

In your journal, reflect on your spiritual values.

- What are they?
- How do you regularly affirm them?
- How are they integrated into your life, your work, your home, and your role in the community?
- Are there areas that you should be consciously re-addressing?
- When was the last time you read or wrote a poem, or spent some quiet quality time on your own?

Consider how you can create a safe basket of unconditional love where you and those around you can grow and be nurtured.

Now for your final activity!

12.6 Activity: Re-evaluate Your Viewpoint

Revisit what you intended to achieve when embarking on this course. Consider what insights and progress you have made and where you plan to go from here. Re-evaluate yourself on the Viewpoint Rating scale. In what areas have you grown and would you like to continue to grow in the future?

Viewpoint Rating:
Your Current Skill and Awareness Levels

	1	2	3	4	5
	Low				High

Assertiveness

Beliefs

Communication

Conflict resolution

Creativity

Decision-making

Deductive thinking

Emotional awareness

Environmental awareness

Ethical guide

Financial management

Focus of attention

Goal-setting

Global perspective

Health

Inductive thinking

Initiative

Interpersonal skills

Motivation

Negotiating skills

Nutrition

Rational thinking

Self-esteem

Sense of purpose

Sense of self

Sensuality

Spiritual awareness

Social awareness

Time management

Values

Vision

We have reached the end of this stage of our journey together. I trust that it has been of benefit and has helped you to become more aware of your identity and enhanced your perception of yourself and your role in the world around you. I wish you all the best for your future travels. If you would like to have further guided support, please contact me at info@colleensullivan.net.

Bon voyage!

Colleen

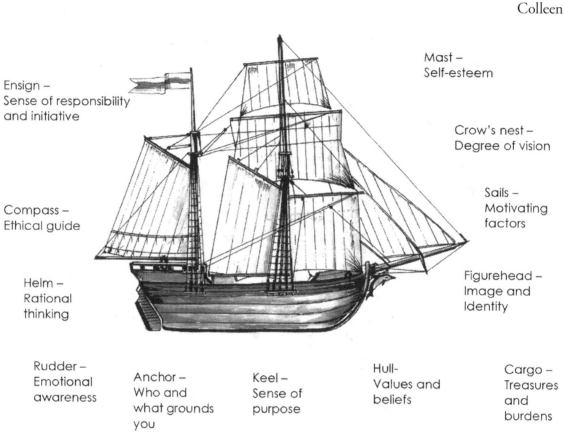

Ensign –
Sense of responsibility
and initiative

Mast –
Self-esteem

Crow's nest –
Degree of vision

Compass –
Ethical guide

Sails –
Motivating
factors

Helm –
Rational
thinking

Figurehead –
Image and
Identity

Rudder –
Emotional
awareness

Anchor –
Who and
what grounds
you

Keel –
Sense of
purpose

Hull-
Values and
beliefs

Cargo –
Treasures
and
burdens

Illustrator - Craig Ballantyne   Concepts - Colleen Sullivan

Ensure Life Changes Happen

Aim to do the following to ensure life changes take place:

- Openly admit your life does need something, and to take a look is the first step.
- Be active, responsible and willing to make decisions. A poor decision is better than no decision at all. Procrastination is a great thief of our energy and it often masks a decision already taken.
- Carve out quiet time just for yourself—with no agenda, no deadlines, and no one else's needs impinging on us—to allow creativity to happen.
- Leave the future open. It is enough to simply believe in yourself.
- Understand that true success requires great integrity. The two are synonymous.
- Look honestly at your life and realise that it is nice to be needed, but not at the expense of your health, your happiness and your sanity.
- Forgive yourself for the hurt you have inadvertently caused those you love.
- Reaching out to others facilitates your growth and your recovery from life's knocks. This is particularly important when your own problems appear to be insurmountable, and you feel as though you have reached an impasse. Intimacy is like a drink of fresh water to a worn soul. Even a taste of it can bring forth desert flowers.
- Believe in a positive force greater than yourself. No one can give this spirituality to you: it takes reflection, prayer and meditation to develop a spirituality that is congruent with yourself. As you grow and change, your life takes on a more spiritual quality in spite of yourself.

Recovery and growth is a process and not an event in itself. It took time for you to become who you are and it also takes time and effort to change.

Craig Ballantyne

Colleen Sullivan

Desiderata

    Go placidly amid the noise and haste, and remember what peace there may be in silence.

    As far as possible, without surrender, be on good terms with all persons. Speak your truth quietly and clearly; and listen to others, even to the dull and the ignorant; they too have their story. Avoid loud and aggressive persons; they are vexations to the spirit.

    If you compare yourself with others you may become vain or bitter, for always there will be greater and lesser persons than yourself. Enjoy your achievements as well as your plans. Keep interested in your career, however humble; it is a real possession in the changing fortunes of time.

    Exercise caution with your business affairs: for the world is full of trickery. But let this not blind you to what virtue there is; many persons strive for high ideals, and everywhere life is full of heroism.

    Be yourself. Especially do not feign affection. Neither be cynical about love; for in the face of all adversity and disenchantment it is as perennial as the grass. Take kindly the counsel of the years, gracefully surrendering the things of youth.

    Nurture strength of spirit to shield you in sudden misfortune. But do not distress yourself with dark imaginings. Many fears are born of fatigue and loneliness.

    Beyond a wholesome discipline be gentle with yourself.

    You are a child of the universe, no less than the trees and the stars; you have a right to be here. And whether or not it is clear to you, no doubt the universe is unfolding as it should.

    Therefore, be at peace with God, whatever you conceive Him to be. And whatever your labors and aspirations, in the noisy confusion of life, keep peace within your soul. With all its sham, drudgery, and broken dreams, it is still a beautiful world.

    Be cheerful, strive to be happy.

—*Max Ehrmann*

References

Antonovsky, Aaron. 1979. *Health, Stress, and Coping*. San Francisco: Jossey-Bass Publishers.
1987. *Unraveling the Mystery of Health*. San Francisco: Jossey-Bass Publishers.
1991. "The Structural Sources of Salutogenic Strengths." In *Personality and Stress: Individual Differences in the Stress Process*, edited by Cary L. Cooper and Roy Payne, 68–104. New York: John Wiley and Sons Ltd.

Appley, Mortimer H. and Richard Trumbull, eds. 1986. *Dynamics of Stress: Physiological, Psychological, and Social Perspectives*. New York: Plenum Press.

Arsenault, André, Shimon L. Dolan, and Marie Reine Van Ameringen. 1991. "Stress and Mental Strain in Hospital Work: Exploring the Relationship Beyond Personality." *Journal of Organisational Behaviour* 12 (6): 483-493.

Australian Government (2008) Understanding Money. How to make it work for you Department of the Treasury. Canberra

Australian Government National Health and Medical Research Council. "Australia and New Zealand." Nutrient Reference Values. http://www.nrv.gov.au.

Australian Government National Health and Medical Research Council. "Australian Dietary Guidelines." Eat for Health. http://www.eatforhealth.gov.au.

Australian Government National Health and Medical Research Council. "Health Information – Australian Dietary Guidelines" http://www.nhmrc.gov.au

Ashford, Susan J. 1988. "Individual Strategies for Coping with Stress During Organizational Transitions." *Journal of Applied Behavioural Science* 24 (1): 19–36.

Bendix, Sonia. 1989. *Industrial Relations in South Africa*. Cape Town: Cedar Press.

Bienvenu, Millard J. 1971. "An Interpersonal Communications Inventory." *Journal of Communication* 21 (4): 381-88.

Blau, Gary J., and Kimberly B. Boal. 1987. "Conceptualizing How Job Involvement and Organizational Commitment Affect Turnover and Absenteeism." *Academy of Management Review* 12 (2): 288–300.

Brennan, Barbara Ann. 1993. *Light Emerging*. New York: Bantam Books.

Bruyere, Rosalyn L. 1994. *Wheels of Light*. New York: Fireside.

Calise, Angela K. 1993. "WC Mental-Stress Claims Decline." *National Underwriter* 97 (35): 3–31.

Cameron, Julia. 1992. *The Artist's Way: A Spritual Path to Higher Creativity*. New York: G. P. Putnam's Sons.

Canau, E., and Gon, S. 1994. "Compensation for Occupational Injuries and Diseases Act." *People Dynamics* 5: 1–4.

Cannon, Walter Bradford. 1939. *The Wisdom of the Body*. New York: W. W. Norton.

Capacchione, Lucia. 1990. *The Picture of Health*. Santa Monica: Hay House.

Carson, Robert Charles, James N. Butcher, and James C. Colman. 1988. *Abnormal Psychology and Modern Life,* 8th ed. Glenview, Illinois: Scott, Forsman and Co.

Carsons, I. 1972. "What Are the Causes of Executive Stress?" *International Management* 27: 16–19.

Carter, Rita. 2009. *The Brain Book: An Illustrated Guide to Its Structure, Function, and Disorders.* Melbourne: Dorling Kindersley Limited.

Cascio, Wayne F. 1989. *Managing Human Resources.* New York: McGraw-Hill International Editions.

Clark, K. 2012. *Introduction to Nutrition Learning Guide.* Sydney: Nature Care College.

Cobb, S. 1974. "Physiological Changes in Men Whose Jobs Were Abolished." *Journal of Psychosomatic Research* 18: 245-258.

Cooper, Cary L., and Marilyn J. Davidson. 1982. "The High Cost of Stress on Woman Managers." *Organizational Dynamics* 10 (4): 44–53.

Cooper, Cary L., and Valerie J. Sutherland. 1992. "The Stress of the Executive Lifestyle: Trends in the 1990s" (survey of European CEOs). *Management Decision* 30 (6): 64–68.

Covey, Stephen R. 1989. *The 7 Habits of Highly Successful People.* New York: Simon and Schuster.

Cox, Tom. 1978. *Stress.* London: Macmillan.

Csikszentmihalyi, Mihaly. 1997. *Creativity.* New York: Harper Perennial.

De Board, Robert. 1983. *Counselling People at Work.* Aldershot, England: Gower.

Edwards, Betty. 1989. *Drawing on the Right Side of the Brain.* Los Angeles: Tarcher Perigee.

Eisenstat, Russell A., and Felner, Robert D. 1984. "Toward a Differentiated View of Burnout: Personal and Organizational Mediators of Job Satisfaction and Stress." *American Journal of Community Psychology* 12 (4): 411–430.

Fleming, Raymond, Andrew Baum, and Jerome E. Singer. 1984. "Toward an Integrative Approach to Study Stress." *Journal of Personality and Social Psychology* 46 (4): 939–949.

Folkman, S. 1984. "Personal Control and Stress and Coping Processes: A Theoretical Analysis." *Journal of Personality and Social Psychology* 46 (40): 839–852.

Frankenhaeuser, Marianne, and Gunn Johansson. 1986. "Stress at Work: Psychobiological and Psychological Aspects." *International Review of Applied Psychology* 35 (3): 287–299.

Frankl, Viktor Emil. 1970. *Man's Search for Meaning.* New York: Washington Square Press.

Fransella, Fay, Richard Bell, and Don Bannister. 2004. *A Manual for Repertory Grid Technique.* West Sussex, England: John Wiley and Sons Ltd.

French, John R. P., Jr., and R. D. Caplan. 1973. "Organizational Stress and Individual Strain." In *The Failure of Success*, edited by Alfred J. Marrow. New York: American Management Association.

French, John R. P., Jr., and Robert L. Kahn. 1962. "A Programmatic Approach to Studying the Industrial Environment and Mental Health." *Journal of Social Issues* 18 (3): 1–47.
1974. "Person-Role Fit." In *Occupational Stress*, edited by Alan A. McLean. Springfield: Charles C. Thomas Publisher, Ltd.

Friedman, Meyer, Ray H. Rosenman, and Vernice Carroll. 1958. "Changes in the Serum Cholesterol and Blood Clotting Time in Men Subjected to Cyclic Variations of Occupational Stress." *Circulation* 17: 852–861.

Furnham, A. 1984. "The Protestant Work Ethic: A Review of the Psychological Literature." *European Journal of Social Psychology* 14 (1): 87–109.

Fuslier, Marcelline R., Daniel C. Ganster, and Bronston T. Mayes. 1987. "Effects of Social Support, Role Stress, and Locus of Control." *Journal of Management* 13 (3): 517–528.

Gecham, Arthur S. 1974. "Without Work, Life Goes." *Journal of Occupational Medicine* 16 (11): 749–751.

Gherman E. M. 1981. *Stress and the Bottom Line: A Guide to Personal Well-Being and Corporate Health*. New York: Amacom.

Glenn, M. 1992. *Senior Management Perceptions of Actions to Support Post Training Utilisation of Leadership and Management Training and Education*. Ann Arbor: University Microfilms International.

Gottlieb, Benjamin H. 1983. *Social Support Strategies*. Beverly Hills: Sage Publications.

Greenhalgh, Trisha. 1993. "Keep Away from the Edge." *Accountancy* 111 (1194): 61.

Greenhaus, Jeffrey H. 1994. *Career Management*. Fort Worth: Dryden Press.

Greenhaus, Jeffrey H., Arthur G. Bedeian, and Kevin W. Mossholder. 1987. "Work Experiences, Job Performance, and Feelings of Personal and Family Well-Being." *Journal of Vocational Behaviour* 31: 200-215.

Greenwood, James W. 1979. *Managing Executive Stress: A Systems Approach*. New York: Wiley and Sons.

Hanna, Thomas. 1988. *Somatics*. Canada: Perseus Books Group.

Harris, Thomas A. 1967. *I'm OK, You're OK: A Practical Guide to Transactional Analysis*. New York: Harper Row.

Hill, Norman C. 1981. *Counseling at the Workplace*. New York: McGraw-Hill.

Hobfoll, Stevan E. 1988. "Conservation of Resources: A New Attempt at Conceptualizing Stress." *American Psychologist* 44 (3): 513–524.

Holland, John L. 1973. *Making Vocational Choices: A Theory of Careers*. New Jersey: Prentice-Hall.

Hollis, James. 1993. *The Middle Passage: From Misery to Meaning in Midlife*. Toronto: Inner City Books.

Homes, Thomas H., and Richard H. Raphe. 1967. "The Social Readjustment Scale." *Journal of Psychosomatic Research* 11 (2): 213–218.

Hurrell, Joseph J., Lawrence R. Murphy, Steven L. Sauter, and Cary L. Copper. (1988). *Occupational Stress: Issues and Developments in Research*. New York: Taylor and Francis.

Isaacson B. I. 1981. *Social Accounting: Qualification and Disclosure: Technical Report*. Cape Town: University of Cape Town.

Isabella, Lynn A. 1988. "The Effect of Career Stage on the Meaning of Key Organizational Events." *Journal of Organisational Behavior* 9 (4): 345–358.

Ivancevich, John M., and Daniel C. Ganster. 1987. *Job Stress: From Theory to Suggestion*. New York: Haworth Press.

Ivancevich, John M., Robert Konopaske, and Michael T. Matteson. 1990. *Organizational Behavior and Management*. Boston: R. R. Donnelley and Sons Company.

Jensen, Uffe Juul, and Gavin Mooney. 1990. *Changing Values in Medical and Health Care Decision Making*. Chichester, England: John Wiley and Sons.

John, R., P. French, and R. D. Caplan. 1970. "Psychosocial Factors in Coronary Heart Disease." *Journal of Industrial Medicine* (September): 383–397.

Jones, John W. 1982. *The Burnout Syndrome: Current Research, Theory, and Interventions*. Illinios: London House Press.

————. 1988. "Breaking the Vicious Stress Cycle (Relationship Between Stress and Accidents)." *Best's Review* (March): 74–76.

Jung, Carl G. 1964. *Man and His Symbols*. London: Aldus Books Limited.

Karasek, Robert, and Töres Therorell. 1990. *Healthy Work: Stress, Productivity, and the Reconstruction of Working Life*. New York: Basic Books.

Katz, Daniel, and Robert Kahn. 1978. *The Social Psychology of Organizations*, 2nd ed. New York: John Wiley and Sons.

Kaufman Harold G. 1982. *Professionals in Search of Work: Coping with the Stress of Job Loss and Underemployment*. New York: John Wiley and Sons.

Kerlinger, Fred N. 1988. *Foundations of Behavioral Research*, 3rd ed. Hong Kong: Holt, Rinehart and Winston, Inc.

Kobasa, Suzanne C. 1979. "Stressful Life Events, Personality, and Health: An Inquiry into Hardiness." *Journal of Personality and Social Psychology* 37 (1): 1–11.

Kobasa, Suzanne C., Salvatore R. Maddi, and Stephen Kahn. 1982. "Hardiness and Health: A Prospective Study." *Journal of Personality and Social Psychology* 42 (1): 168–177.

Kohn, Melvin L., and Carmi Schooler. 1983. *Work and Personality: An Inquiry into the Impact of Social Stratification*. Norwood: Ablex Publishing Co.

Krantz, D. S., and S. E. Raisen. 1988. "Environmental Stress, Reactivity and Ischaemic Heart Disease." *British Journal of Medical Psychology* 61 (1): 3–16.

Krantz, James. 1985. "Group Process Under Conditions of Organizational Decline." *Journal of Applied Behavioral Science* 21(1): 1–17.

Kreider, J. R. 1986. "Stress Claims Can Be Stressful (Accepting Stress Claims Are Work Related)." *Best's Review* 87: 66-70.

Lazarus, Richard S. 1966. *Psychological Stress and the Coping Process*. New York: McGraw-Hill.
————. 1984. *Psychology and Health*. Washington D.C.: American Psychological Association.

LaRocco, James M., James S. House, and John R. P. French Jr. 1980. "Social Support, Occupational Stress, and Health." *Journal of Health and Social Behavior* 21 (3): 202–218

Latack, Janina C. 1981. "Person/Role Conflict: Holland's Model Extended to Role-Stress Research, Stress Management, and Career Development." *Academy of Management Review* 6 (1): 89–103.

Levi, Lennart. 1984. *Stress in Industry: Causes, Effects, and Prevention*. Geneva: International Labour Office.

Levitan, Sar A. and Clifford M. Johnson. 1982. *Second Thoughts on Work*. Michigan: Upjohn Institute of Unemployment Research.

Lewis, L. 1993. "Employers Place More Emphasis on Managing Employee Stress (to Lower Medical and Psychiatric Claims)." *Business and Health* 2: 46–48.

Luft, Joseph. 1982. *The Johari Window: A Graphic Model of Awareness in Interpersonal Relations*. Arlington, VA: NTL Institute

Machlowitz, Marilyn. 1980. *Workaholics: Living with Them, Working with Them*. Reading: Addison-Wesley.

　　　1983. *Determining the Effects of Work—Alcoholism*. Ann Arbor: University Microfilms International.

Mager, Robert, and P. Pipe. 1979. *Criterion-Referenced Instruction*, 2nd ed. Mager Associates, Inc.

Malik, M. S. 1993. "All Dressed Up and No Place to Go." *Modern Office Technology* 38 (2): 27–28.

Maslow, Abraham H. 1954. *Motivation and Personality*. New York: Harper.

Matthes, Karen. 1992. "In Pursuit of Leisure: Employees Want More Time Off." *HR Focus* 69 (5): 1–7.

Maturi, R. 1992. "Stress Can Be Beaten." *Industry Week* 241 (14): 22–26.

McLean, Alan A. 1970. *Mental Health in Work Organizations*. Chicago: Rand McNally.

McClelland, David C. 2000. *Human Motivation*. Cambridge, England: Cambridge University Press.

McGuigan, Frank J. 1968. *Experimental Psychology: A Methodological Approach*, 2nd ed. Upper Saddle River, NJ: Prentice-Hall.

McGuire, Michelle, and Kathy A. Beerman. 2011. *Nutritional Sciences: From Fundamentals to Food*. Belmont, CA: Wadsworth Cengage Learning.

"Mental Stress Claims Show Decline." 1993. *Occupational Hazards* 55 (10): 61-62.

Metcalf, C. W., and Roma Felible. 1992. "Humor: An Antidote for Terminal Professionalism." *Industry Week* 241 (14): 14–19.

Mortimer, Jeylan T., and Kathryn M. Borman. 1988. *Work Experience and Psychological Development Through the Life Span*. Colorado: Westview Press Inc.

Murphy, Lawrence R. 1989. "Workplace Interventions for Stress Reduction and Prevention." In *Causes, Coping, and Consequences of Stress at Work*, edited by Cary L. Cooper and Roy Payne. Chichester, England: Wiley.

Near, Janet P. 1987. "Work and Nonwork Correlates of the Career Plateau." *Academy of Management Proceedings* (August): 380–384.

Neff, Walter S. 1977. *Work and Human Behavior*. Chicago: Aldine.

Newton, T. J., and A. Keenan. 1990. "The Moderating Effect of the Type A Behavior Pattern and Locus of Control Upon the Relationship Between Change in Job Demands and Change in Psychological Strain." *Human Relations* 43 (12): 1229–1255.

Overman, Stephenie, and Linda Thornburg. 1992. "Beating the Odds." *HR Magazine* 37 (3): 42–47.

Paffenberger, J. H. 1988. "Exercise and Health." *S. A. Joernaal van Voortgesette Mediese Onderring* 6: 28.

Parker, Donald F., and Thomas A. DeCotiis. 1983. "Organizational Determinants of Job Stress." *Organizational Behavior and Human Performance* 32, 160-177.

Payne, Roy L., Muayyad M. Jabri, and Alan W. Pearson. 1988. "On the Importance of Knowing the Affective Meaning of Job Demands." *Journal of Organizational Behavior* 9 (2): 149–158.

Pearline, Leonard I., Morton A. Lieberman, Elizabeth G. Meneghan, and Joseph T. Mullan. 1981. "The Stress Process." *Journal of Health and Social Behavior* 22 (4): 337–356.

Potter-Efron, Ronald T. 2005. *Handbook of Anger Management: Individual, Couple, Family, and Group Approaches.* New York: Haworth Press

Price, Virginia A. 1982. "What Is Type A? A Cognitive Social Learning Model." *Journal of Occupational Behavior* 3 (1): 109–129.

Raelin, Joe. 1984. "An Examination of Deviant/Adaptive Behavior in the Organizational Careers of Professionals." *Academy of Management Review* 9 (3): 423-427.

"Resource Sheet: Anger Management." 2007. Cancer Institute, NSW.

Robbins, Stephen P. 1986. *Organizational Behavior,* 3rd ed. Upper Saddle River, NJ: Prentice-Hall.

Rosenau, Douglas E. 2002. *A Celebration of Sex.* Nashville: Thomas Nelson, Inc.

Roskies, Ethel. 1987. *Stress Management for the Healthy Type A: Theory and Practice.* New York: Guilford Press.

Saleh, Shoukry D., and K. Desai. 1990. "An Empirical Analysis of Job Stress and Job Satisfaction of Engineers." *Journal of Engineering and Technology Management* 7 (1): 37–48.

Samy, Ama. 2005. *Zen: Awakening to Your Original Face.* Chennai, India: Cre-A Publishers.

Seyle, Hans. 1978. *The Stress of My Life.* New York: McGraw-Hill.

Scarfalloto, Rudy. 1997. *The Alchemy of Opposites.* Las Vegas: New Falcon Publications.

Schafer, Walter. 1987. *Stress Management for Wellness.* New York: Holt, Rinehart and Winston, Inc.

Schein, E. H. 1980. *Organizational Psychology,* 3rd ed. Englewood Cliffs, NJ: Prentice-Hall.

Schepers, J. M. 1992. *Toetskonstruksie: Teorie en Praktyk.* Johannesburg: Rand Afrikaans University.

Schuler, Randall. 1982. "An Integrative Transactional Process Model of Stress in Organizations." *Journal of Occupational Behavior* 3 (1): 5–19.

Schut, J. H. 1992. "From the Folks Who Brought You the Hot Tub ..." *Institutional Investor* 26 (11): 171.

Self NutritionData. "Nutritional Effects of Food Processing." *Self.* http://nutritiondata.self.com/topics/processing.

Shapiro, Frances. 2001. *Eye Movement Desensitization and Reprocessing (EMDR): Basic Principles, Protocols, and Procedures.* New York: Guilford Press.

    2008. *The EMDR Approach to Psychotherapy.* Watsonville, CA: The EMDR Institute.

Short, Joseph, and Gavriel Salvendy. 1982. "Occupational Stress: Review and Reappraisal." *Human Factors* 24 (2): 129-162.

Siegel, Bernie S. 1990. *Peace, Love, and Healing.* New York: Harper and Row.

Siegel, Daniel. 2007. *The Mindful Brain: Reflection and Attunement in the Cultivation of Well-Being.* New York: Harper and Row.

Siegman, Aron W., and Theodore M. Dembroski, eds. 1989. *In Search of Coronary-Prone Behavior: Beyond Type A.* New Jersey: L. Erlbaum Associates.

Slaney, R. B., and J. C. Russell. 1987. "Perspectives on Vocational Behaviour, 1986: A Review." *Journal of Vocational Behavior* 31: 111–173.

Solomon, Charlene Marmer. 1993. "If You Feel Overworked, Just Think About How the Japanese Must Feel." *Personnel Journal* 72 (6): 58.

Spector, Paul E. 1982. "Behavior in Organizations as a Function of Employee's Locus of Control." *Psychological Bulletin* 91 (3): 482–497.

Spielberger, Charles D., and Irwin G. Sarason. 1986. *Stress and Anxiety*. Washington: Hemisphere Publishing Corporation.

Stein, Nancy L., Bennett Leventhal, and Tom Trabasso, eds. 1990. *Psychological and Biological Approaches to Emotion*. Hillsdale, NJ: Lawrence Eribaum Associates.

Steptoe, Andrew. 1981. *Psychological Factors in Cardiovascular Disorders*. New York: Academic Press.

1991. "Psychological Coping and Physiological Stress Responses." In *Personality and Stress: Individual Differences in the Stress Process*, edited by Cary L. Cooper and Roy Payne. New York: John Wiley and Sons Ltd.

Steptoe, Andrew, and A. Appels. 1989. *Stress, Personal Control, and Health*. Chichester, England: Wiley.

Stout, Suzanne K., Slocum, John W., and Cron, William L. 1988. "Dynamics of the Career Plateauing Process." *Journal of Vocational Behavior* 32 (1): 74–91.

Stumpf, Stephen A., and Robinowitz, Samuel. 1981. "Career Stage as a Moderator of Performance Relationships with Facets of Job Satisfaction and Role Perceptions." *Journal of Vocational Behavior* 18 (2): 202–18.

Strümpfer, D. J. W. 1992a. *Psychological Strengths as Point of Departure: Fortigensis*. Stellenbosch: Psychological Association of South Africa.

1992b. *A Study of the Factors Related to Psychological Strength in a Sample of First-Line Supervisors*. Cape Town: The Institute of Research Development, Human Sciences Research Council.

Tang, Thomas Li-Ping and Monty L. Hammantree. 1992. "The Effects of Hardiness, Police Stress, and Life Stress on Police Officers' Illness and Absenteeism." *Public Personnel Management* 21 (4): 493–510.

Thomas, Kenneth Wayne, and Ralph H. Kilmann. 2002. Thomas-Kilmann Conflict Mode Instrument. UK: Pennwood.

University of Sydney. "Glycemic Index." http://www.glycemicindex.com

van der Post, Laurens. 2010. *The Lost World of the Kalahari*. Orlando, FL: Harcourt Brace and Company.

von Bertalanffy, L. 1974. "General Systems Theory." In *American Handbook of Psychiatry* Vol. 1, 2nd. ed., edited by Silvano Arieti. New York: Basic Books.

Vroom,Victor H. 1962. "Ego-Involvement, Job Satisfaction, and Job Performance." *Personnel Psychology* 15 (2): 159–177.

Wall, R., and I. D. Nicholas. 1985. "Health Care Costs Getting to the Heart of the Problem— Stress." *Journal of Risk Management* 32: 20–22.

Wahlqvist, Mark L. 2002. *Food and Nutrition*. Singapore: South Wind Productions.

Weber, Max. 1947. *The Theory of Social and Economic Organization.* Translated by A. M. Henderson and T. Paterson. Edited by T. Paterson. New York: Free Press.

Whitney, Eleanor Noss, Sharon Rady Rolfes, Tim Crowe, David Cameron-Smith, and Adam Walsh. 2011. *Understanding Nutrition: Australian and New Zealand Edition.* South Melbourne, Australia: Cengage Learning.

Wilson Schaef, Anne. 1998. *Living in Process.* New York: Ballantine Publishing Group.

Winett, Richard Allen, Abby C. King, and David G. Altman. 1989. *Health Psychology and Public Health: An Integrative Approach.* New York: Pergamon Press.

Websites

Business Analysis Made Easy
http://www.business-analysis-made-easy.com

"Calculator," Nutrient Reference Values for Australia and New Zealand, NHMRC
http://www.nrv.gov.au/calculator/calculator.htm

CHOICE Online
http://www.choice.com.au

"Decision Matrix," ASQ.
http://asq.org/learn-about-quality/decision-making-tools/overview/decision-matrix.html

FoodChoices
http://www.foodchoices.com.au

Food Standards Australia New Zealand
http://www.foodstandards.gov.au

Global Agewatch Index
http://www.helpage.org/global-agewatch/popultion-ageing-data

Glycemic Index Foundation
http://www.gisymbol.com.au

Heart Foundation
http://www.heartfoundation.org.au

Micronutrient Information Center. Linus Pauling Institute, Oregon State University
http://lpi.oregonstate.edu/infocenter/phytochemicals.html

MoneySmart, Australia Securities and Investment Commission
http://www.moneysmart.gov.au

PubMed, US National Library of Medicine, National Institutes of Health
http://www.ncbi.nlm.nih.gov/pubmed

"Understanding Stress," The Wholistic Development Exchange
http://www.wholisticdev.com/Stress-Management-Tips.shtml

"VIA Me! Character Strengths Profile"
http://www.viame.org/survey/Account/Register

Activities	Date Completed
1.1	
1.2	
1.3	
1.4	
2.1	
2.2	
2.3	
2.4	
2.5	
2.6	
2.7	
2.8	
2.9	
3.1	
3.2	
3.3	
3.4	
3.5	
3.6	
3.7	
4.1	
4.2	
4.3	

Activities	Date Completed
4.4	
4.5	
4.6	
4.7	
4.8	
5.1	
5.2	
5.3	
5.4	
5.5	
5.6	
5.7	
6.1	
6.2	
6.3	
6.4	
6.5	
6.6	
6.7	
6.8	
6.9	
6.10	
6.11	
7.1	

Activities	Date Completed
7.2	
7.3	
7.4	
7.5	
7.6	
7.7	
7.8	
8.1	
8.2	
8.3	
8.4	
8.5	
8.6	
8.7	
9.1	
9.2	
9.3	
9.4	
9.5	
9.6	
9.7	
9.8	
10.1	
10.2	

Activities	Date Completed
10.3	
10.4	
10.5	
10.6	
11.1	
11.2	
11.3	
11.4	
11.5	
11.6	
11.7	
12.1	
12.2	
12.3	
12.4	
12.5	
12.6	

Printed in the United States
by Baker & Taylor Publisher Services